# Bittersweet

Books by Mary Summer Rain

**Nonfiction**

*Spirit Song*
*Phoenix Rising*
*Dreamwalker*
*Phantoms Afoot*
*Earthway*
*Daybreak*
*Soul Sounds*
*Whispered Wisdom*
*Ancient Echoes*
*Bittersweet*

**Fiction**

*The Seventh Mesa*

**Children's**

*Mountains, Meadows and Moonbeams*

# Bittersweet

## Mary Summer Rain

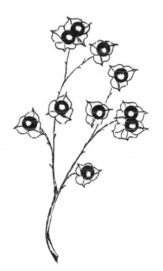

HAMPTONROADS
PUBLISHING COMPANY, INC.

Cover design by Jonathan S. Friedman

For information write:

Hampton Roads Publishing Company, Inc.
976 Norfolk Square
Norfolk, VA 23502

Or call: (804)459-2453
FAX: (804)455-8907

If you are unable to order this book from your local
bookseller, you may order directly from the publisher.
Quantity discounts for organizations are available.
Call 1-800-766-8009, toll-free.

ISBN 1-57174-032-5

10 9 8 7 6 5 4 3 2 1

Printed on acid-free paper in Canada

*For those who carry a bough*
*of bittersweet within their hearts.*

# AUTHOR'S FOREWORD

After I published *Soul Sounds,* my first journal, readership response was overwhelmingly appreciative. This predominant sentiment warmed my heart and underscored the wisdom of those who urged me to publish it. Not only did the public gain insights from my daily life, it finally saw me in the light of the common person that I am—I scrub toilets too. And my correspondents, through various means of subtle persuasion, placed their gentle requests for a second journal. They wished to be kept abreast of my activities, the family, and special friends I'd introduced them to.

So then, though I had been convinced that I'd never expose those very personal issues to the public eye again, I've since learned to never say never. I took the wishes of my readers to heart and had six hundred pages of a second journal typed up in manuscript form before I began having serious doubts about publishing it. These doubts prompted the need to have an unbiased individual read it for an opinion, and the verdict was not favorable. The reason for it underscored my own inner feeling that nobody would believe it all. This individual feared that my credibility would suffer if the journal went public. Veracity is an attribute I cherish and hold close to my heart. And though I knew some of the events I'd recorded appeared too incredible to believe, I still recorded them as they happened. Therefore, when these strange events began manifesting in a frequent pattern, accumulating one after the other, like a long string of rare pearls, they appeared too extraordinary for the mind to perceive. . .and I tore the manuscript into tiny pieces and burned them. A second journal was definitely not coming from me.

Yet the concept of publishing another journal was continually spearing through my consciousness. The relentless thought would not give me a moment's peace until I accepted that the twelfth book would be the manifestation of this bittersweet situation—a situation of doing a book I was reluctant to do but couldn't not do. And, in order to appease the former objection to the material, I would compromise by making this one different. It would not be arranged in the format of a daily diary as the first one was, it would be marked by the more outstanding events in my life. In this manner, the mundane aspects of my life have been left out and, instead, *Bittersweet* focuses on the main events that have transpired since *Soul Sounds* ended.

I've titled each of these separate events. Therefore, I suppose this format transforms the second journal into a collection of short stories rather than a day-by-day diary. And as I scanned the varying content of these separate stories, it struck me that I've come full circle. Book Number One began in a simple mountain log cabin and, by the end of Book Number Twelve, another tiny mountain dwelling nestled among the high pines becomes my mainstay.

Changes. Always so many changes. Every moment we breathe, multitudes of fragmented aspects coalesce from the stuff of probabilities into their final manifested form of a physical event. This then becomes our reality. What we do with these manifested realities is a small portion of who we are. *Bittersweet* is, therefore, my heartfelt Giveaway to you. On this snowy winter morn I open my heart and offer you a bouquet of bittersweet. . .the bouquet of my life.

Due to the sensitivity of some stories, various participants' names have been changed. These are marked by an asterisk the first time they are mentioned.

It is suggested that, for continuity, the stories be read in order. Though the format is not in diary form, *Bittersweet* constitutes a life journal and events have been recorded chronologically.

# TABLE OF CONTENTS

## 1992

## 1993

# 1994

# Bittersweet

# 1992

# GRAND CENTRAL STATION

By January of 1992, we'd been living in our rental house for several years. The "we" I speak of is my immediate family consisting of my husband Bill, myself and our three daughters, Jenny, Aimee, and Sarah. With us for many years was also our extended family, our long-time friend, Robin, and her daughter Mandy.

The rental house I speak of rests atop a heavily-treed hillcrest at 9,500 ft. elevation beside Pikes Peak. The house, years ago, was once a ski lodge. Remnants of those past times remain today. Rustic wooden signs naming the various runs are still affixed to the trees. The cleared ski trails still veer off in many different directions; only now, young aspens have sprouted to reclaim their territory. And, directly behind the house, gutted and empty high voltage boxes peek their square metal lids out of the ground like half-buried coffins. Towering above these, the remains of the gear mechanism stand frozen in time, never again turning to pull a busy tow line.

Silent gears. Ghostly trails. Empty voltage casements. Faded trail signs pointing the way to nowhere. Nothing viable left but the lodge that seven people now called home.

Home. Home was in the shape of two A-frames positioned in a tee configuration. One was the main lodge with a stone and knotty pine living room that came equipped with an enormous stone fireplace. The raised hearth provided seating in a semi-circle around a roaring fire. The kitchen area was located at the far end of the living room and was separated by a built-in bookcase and two steps up. Off the kitchen was a half bath. Above the living room was an open loft with a hallway leading to a back bedroom and bath.

The second A-frame portion consisted of a large room on the ground floor. This room had kitchen facilities and a full bath. Above, again, there was an open loft that led to a bath and a second bedroom.

With only two bedrooms, we managed to arrange the seven of us so everyone was reasonably satisfied. Sarah and Aimee shared the loft above the main living room and Robin and Mandy shared the back bedroom. All four utilized the bath between their rooms. Jenny took the other loft while we were in the second bedroom. The living area below Jenny was entirely converted into office space for Bill and me, for we required the space for our two desks, warehouse room for the stock of children's books we were self-publishing and a separate ship-ping area for these. Finally, a laundry room was located between the two A-frames and, from there, a large shop area led out to the garage.

I realize that, in describing the layout of this house, it sounds like an enormous structure. It wasn't. The upper floor of an A-frame is small due to the slanted walls of the roof. The girls didn't have much privacy due to the open loft and large upper windows.

Bill and I would begin our business day while Jenny was still trying to sleep above us. We all made sacrifices to make it work. We did what we had to do in order to share expenses.

Bill and I had our work which, most times, lasted until after dinner. Robin worked full time in Woodland Park; Aimee did too. Sarah and Mandy were in school all day. And Jenny managed the house by fixing the meals and doing the laundry for us all.

The house was not huge, but it did have its idiosyncrasies in the layout. If you entered the blue front door, you could turn right, climb the open loft stairs, pass through Aimee and Sarah's room, make another right into Jenny's loft and descend the second set of open stairs to end up in the office. Our friends who visited us took awhile to find their way through the twists and turns. And everywhere there were hidden cubbyholes and crawlspaces behind the paneling. It was a house with so much personality it became an entity onto itself. It was a place that effortlessly pulled you into its character. So despite our crowded space arrangement, we all loved it.

Perhaps the many cubbies and hidey-holes had something to do with it, or it could be possible that the mountainous location was the reason. Whatever it was, the dwelling began to present us with increasing instances of unusual happenings.

The beginnings were so subtle we gave them no notice. Odd feelings overcame us at different times. A momentary sensation of being watched. Jenny's cat suddenly jumping up and racing from the room. Our dog, Magic, turning her head and growling beneath her breath at nothing we could see.

Then we laughed when several of us, at different times, misplaced items. It became a standing joke about how old we were getting until—until the items began showing up under our noses, like on the carpet in the middle of the living room where everyone walks, or on the kitchen table just after it was cleared from dinner, or atop the newly-made bed in the morning. By this time, things weren't so subtle anymore, yet we still joked about it being some prank-playing spirit. We joked. We joked, yet knew there was no spirit dwelling in the house. It seemed that we were all so busy with our separate lives that we were too preoccupied to give the contradiction serious thought. Maybe we didn't want to.

As time passed, we stopped "misplacing" things and we'd chuckle with comments about us not getting feeble-minded after all. Although it was never voiced, we privately questioned the sudden cessation of lost articles that reappeared, seemingly, of their own volition. So the stage had been set. The atmosphere of unexplained events surrounded us. It had our attention—at least subliminally.

The next stage was focused on Magic who would suddenly turn, spy something invisible to us, and take off chasing it through the house. This always gave the willies to those of us who happened to witness this little cat 'n' mouse game of tag. Yet even this escalated to bolder activities by our unseen visitors. Magic would give hot pursuit and skid to a sliding halt at one of the crawlspace doors just as it. . .slammed shut in her face!

By my side of the bed was one of these doors that led one up and along the length of the house. There was also a trapdoor that let one out onto the roof. I never liked that little door in our bedroom. Nobody else cared much for it either; consequently, it was always locked by a small hook latch.

One sunny afternoon, Robin went to set clean laundry on our bed and was taken aback to find the little door gaping wide open. She closed it, forgetting to tell us of the strange incident until, some days later, one of the girls ran after Magic as she was in pursuit again. Magic raced into our bedroom and, just as her human follower got to the doorway, the little door beside the bed slammed shut. Magic sat there whining like she'd just lost her playmate for the day.

After hearing these two stories, Bill placed a stronger latch on the little door. The incidents continued. What amused me was the fact that Magic stopped her initial growling and, instead, acted as though she were playing with someone very familiar to her. An innocent game of hide and seek. Eventually, her familiarity rubbed off on us. This was how we began to perceive our visitor as a friend rather than some type of force or entity we needed be wary of.

Only with hindsight can we now see how these bits and pieces were presented as a compassionate means of gentle persuasion. They. . . gently, one tiny stage at a time, introduced us to the idea of interacting with members of a family we never knew we had. However, at the time, nobody was openly ready to admit to this possibility until we graduated to the sensory stage. This involved sight and smell and, as it happened, came at a time when it was most noticeable—winter.

When it's cold and snowy, all the windows and doors are shut tight. So where was that fresh air smell coming from? We all smelled it. It was as though someone left a window wide open in the middle of winter. When we checked, nothing was open. Eventually we had to connect the scent with the star visitors because an appearance of some type would always follow on its heels. These appearances were so subtle they were perceived as being subliminal or naturally-occurring ocular phenomena. A splash of white flashing past a doorway in your peripheral vision. When your head snapped around, nothing was there. "Well, of *course* there's nothing there," you mumble to yourself while secretly hoping there really wasn't anything there. And you resume doing whatever you were doing from an adjusted position that gets the doorway out of *any* vision point. Who wants to think they've begun hallucinating? Worse, who wants to admit they really are seeing things playing hide and seek with them in their own house? Me? Nope. Any of us? No way.

But the mind games one uses to rationalize such aberrant events end abruptly when hide and seek turns to peek-a-boo. Now the hair *does* stand on end. Now you freeze in your own smell of fear that rushes from your pores. First comes the now-familiar scent of fresh air, then, a slight movement draws your attention. You look up. You freeze. A small pale face with small eyes is peering around the doorway at you. You're so scared, totally startled. You don't want to believe you just saw what you saw, so you quickly look down. When you're brave enough to test your eyes again and your heart resumes its beating, you keep your head down and ease your sights back to the doorway. . .nothing. Did you really see that little face peering at you? Nah. But wasn't it a *movement* that initially drew your attention to that doorway? Well, yes but. . .It seems that Jenny and I are the only ones in our family who have had this experience. I can't begin to reason why the others haven't. If truth be told, I wouldn't wish this experience on my worst enemy. It's unnerving. Fearfully unnerving. A real heart stopper. It leaves you with the fear of being alone ever again.

As with all things, time lessens the intensity of our experiences. Fears and anxieties wane. And these did fall to the wayside after a spell without any visitations. I say "visitations" because we had no visuals for a while even though the scent still came and went on a routine basis.

So, I figured, the peek-a-boo bit stopped because they didn't want to keep scaring us. Once visual evidence was presented to at least a couple of us, that was all that was necessary. This idea soothed my mind, yet I was to discover that the reprieve was only a pause between breaths.

The next stage was light. Light flooding the front loft bedroom window in the wee hours of the morning. A bright ray of light that came down through the window. The ray was all anyone could remember of the incident. . .on that night I couldn't sleep and went down on the living room couch—below the loft.

I'd finally drifted off to sleep when I subliminally heard the front door open behind me. No way, I recall thinking. Magic hadn't even stirred. She was asleep on the floor beside the couch. She would've barked like crazy if somebody had opened that door. I must've dreamed the sound. That's what I remember thinking until I smelled fresh air. What? And then I felt the top and bottom of my coverlet being raised off me. Oh *God!* I sat up and screamed for Sarah, who was up in the loft. No sound came from me—no sound other than air rushing past my throat. The next thing I recall is sitting on the edge of the couch the following morning, head in hands, thinking about the night before. Sarah and Aimee came down for breakfast before work and school. As it turned out, Aimee had seen the bright light come flooding in the front windows the night before. All she recalled thinking at the time was "car lights, just headlights." Yet she knew they couldn't be headlights because we were on a hillcrest and *this* light was shining *down* through the window.

I told the girls of my experience the night before. In the retelling, I thought it curious why, when I sat up to call out, I never saw *who* was at my shoulders and feet holding up the coverlet. In my memory it was as though the blanket had levitated itself. Now I know that the visual of those two beings was blocked from my memory.

We had advanced up to seeing and experiencing the lights. This, after several events, came to correspond with a one-on-one visitation or journey. Some remembered. Others blocked.

When Bill heard of my experience on the couch I could see his gears turning. He wanted to "go for a ride" too. I thought he was nuts. "Go ahead," I said, "sleep on the magic carpet couch tonight if that's what you want." And he did. Only he slept in all his clothes. I wish I'd been given that choice.

The following morning we discussed his night. He'd been so expectant that he'd tossed and turned, checking the clock every hour or so. He relayed an event he thought he'd dreamed. He reasoned that it couldn't have possibly happened because he'd been awake so much. However, when he mentioned that 3 A.M. was the last time he checked the clock, I knew his dream was no dream. He'd felt and seen himself rising up off the couch and thought "this is neat!" and that's all he recalled.

Three o'clock in the morning appears to be at least in our experience—an extremely active time for this type of event to manifest. I had no doubt in my mind that his recall was generated from a real event. When Aimee was questioned about that night she didn't recall any light, but did remember stirring in her sleep and smelling fresh air. She had no idea that her dad had been below her on the couch that night. He hadn't told anyone but me.

Soon the magic couch became a joke—literally—because the bright light began coming through our bedroom window too. To see it was to accept it, and you just closed your eyes until memory was blocked and morning came. Come morning, you were nicely tucked back beneath your blankets again. That action showed us that someone definitely cared.

As the seasons changed, so did the encounters. They became meetings that were usually unannounced. Understandings were reached. Knowledge was shared. Friendships were forged.

One evening, while Bill and I were talking in the living room, we heard the fast approach of a Flight for Life helicopter. The sound quickly became frightening, for it was too close and too low. I raced out our front door just in time to see an unlighted airborne vehicle angle up high to the right and out of sight into the twilight. But just above me—I thought I could touch it if I reached up high enough—was a glowing ball of light silently passing over my head. On its tail was a military helicopter in hot pursuit. I feared it was going to clip the top of the A-frame it was so low. It too flew over my head. I was looking up at its underside.

Everything sped by so fast that, by the time Bill and Sarah got outside, all they could see was the ball of light veer high in the sky and the helicopter fly over the next hillside. We watched the light. It had seemed to stop in the sky. It now appeared to resemble a sparkling star. We kept our eyes on it for a long while, when suddenly Sarah cryptically said, "Look behind us." And there, slowly rising and floating left and right, was another ball of light. We watched that one until it sped out of sight. We went back inside. We were so excited over seeing UFOs and their related escorts, and the sight of the military copter being left in their dust just added to the veracity of the whole event.

While all this was transpiring, Robin had been in the shower. Later, after we told her what had happened, she commented that she'd heard the noise of the helicopter and thought it was going to hit the house. I felt bad that she'd missed everything.

Sometimes, when all I've experienced with our star family becomes too heavy, I find myself using the old defense mechanism of wondering if, after all, I'm just crazy. Yet remembering the night I nearly reached up and touched the ball of light, then saw the underside of the military aircraft, solidifies my sanity. I was not a lone witness. Robin, not knowing what was transpiring, heard the helicopter and, months later, I would find out that people had reported the incident to the local sheriff's office.

Sometimes. Sometimes the things I've seen and heard tend to push me toward denial. It's not real. This is too much to deal with. I can't shoulder all this new incoming information, therefore it's easier to question all of it or pretend none of it happened.

Witnesses. There are others who can bear witness to the events I want to deny.

So much. Too much. Too much to wish away. Tell me. How do you wish it all away after our star relations have transformed your house into their very own Grand Central Station?

# FRIENDLY FIRE

The majority of this story took place in 1992, yet it had its beginnings in the fall of 1991. No mention of the incident was made in the published version of my *Soul Sounds* journal because it was deleted from the manuscript by my attorney. This Virginia Beach attorney, John Hart, was representing twelve authors who were suing three publishers for the purpose of gaining their book rights back. Since we were preparing our case when *Soul Sounds* was ready to go to print, my words had to be carefully censored. Now the incidents can be declassified.

In September of 1991, we had out-of-state friends come to visit us for a few days. One evening, while we lingered over dinner, the conversation shifted to the publishing problems we'd been experiencing. Our visitors, *Tony and *Rosa, were outraged that we'd been put through such stress. They were incredulous over the pain and anguish we were suffering. On a personal level, I'd felt that I'd failed No-Eyes by not protecting her. I'd berated myself over and over for letting someone rip her out of my arms.

As we unveiled the details of events that made us suspicious of what was really happening with my books, our two listeners appeared to have the identical thought at the same time, for curious grins curled their lips as they looked to one another.

"What's so funny?" I asked.

"Nothing's funny," Tony replied. "Go on with your story."

I looked to Bill before giving our guests my attention again. "Well, if nothing's funny, why are you both grinning?"

Rosa's grin grew bigger. "We'll tell you in a minute. We want to hear the rest of your story first."

"There's not much more to tell. We just don't know what to do. The situation's gotten out of hand. Every time we confront the publisher he brushes us off with placating assurances meant to stall us. It's driving me crazy knowing something's terribly wrong and not being able to do anything about it."

"That's where we can help you," Tony responded. "We know someone who can end your problems."

I hated to doubt our friend's word and I was grateful for his concern, yet I couldn't see how anyone could put an end to the situation as it stood. I rolled my eyes. "Well. . .unless this 'someone' is a mobster or an ace attorney, I don't see how anyone can help us."

Their grins grew into wide smiles.

Rosa raised a delicate brow. "Of the two options you mentioned, our friend is *not* the attorney."

Her meaning was loud and clear. It struck us like a bolt of lightning.

Bill and I exchanged glances. I saw the corner of his mouth tip up ever so slightly.

"Bill! That's terrible!"

He shrugged. "*Somebody's* gotta fight for us little guys."

Kiddingly, I slapped his arm. I then addressed our friends in a serious manner. "So. What exactly are you saying here?"

Rosa began to explain. "In Tony's business, he crosses paths with all kinds of people. Some of these have gotten to be more than just passing acquaintances. And one of these owes him a favor."

"A favor," I repeated.

Tony stepped into the conversation. "Mary, what would you say if I told you that whatever you wanted done would be done?"

Things were getting serious. Nobody was grinning anymore. "Come again?" I said.

He gave me a gentle smile. "Okay. Let's see. . .maybe you could envision this guy's book warehouse blown up, or maybe you would think he'd look spiffy in cement shoes. Get the drift?"

I wish I hadn't. It took me awhile to find my voice. "You *are* talking about a mobster! Tony, if I did something like that then I'd owe *them* a favor. Right? Isn't that how it works?"

"Wrong," Rosa interjected. "Well, technically, yes, but weren't you listening? They owe *Tony* one. It would be a returned favor done for *Tony*. You wouldn't even come into the picture."

I was speechless for a minute. "Well, I certainly can't fix my problems *that* way!"

Tony didn't agree. He frowned. "It can work all kinds of ways. It doesn't have to involve any kind of violence. You'd be surprised how many ways these guys can take care of problems."

"Oh sure," I sighed, "like making the publisher an offer he can't refuse."

He grinned. "You got it."

I looked to Rosa. She was smiling.

I looked over at Bill. He was too.

I grinned back at them. "Get outta here. You guys are awful. You're pulling my leg."

Tony's smile vanished. "This is a serious offer, Mary. The law just doesn't work sometimes."

"It's going to have to this time."

Tony sighed heavily. "You have no conception of how the law works. You have no inkling of how this guy's attorneys can rip you apart and gobble you up like pieces of candy."

I recoiled at his words. "Why would they do that?"

Rosa was exasperated with me. "See? See how innocent she is? Honey, they are going to make you look like a crazy person because of your beliefs. They are going to even attack No-Eyes."

I was aghast. "Oh no, she's got nothing to do with this publishing business."

She was getting worked up. "Oh God, Mary, wake up! That's how attorneys operate! They try to make the plaintiffs look like they're crazy or liars or whatever they can hook their claws into. Then they rip and tear. Mary, they *love* ripping and tearing!"

"Why?" I softly asked.

Rosa just sighed.

I looked to Bill. His expression underscored what our friends were saying. I appeared to be the only one in the room that was ignorant to the ways and wiles of attorneys. My voice was low. "They will not touch my No-Eyes. I will defend her to the death."

Tony's voice matched my own. "You can't win against them, you know. You can't win against them unless you have the mind of an attorney. You don't. You can't play by their rules. It isn't in you."

I glared at him. "I may not have their devious mind, but I have truth on my side. I can mentally tangle with the best of them."

"That's true," he softly admitted, "but in that process of doing verbal battle with them, No-Eyes will still be dragged through the muck. They'll still get their two-cents in. They'll still get their aspersions cast her way. They'll have their say anyway. Whether you counter with the truth won't matter after their ugly assumptions and speculations are already publicly voiced."

I thought on that. "That's a chance I'll have to take. Battles come in all forms. Now that I know what they'll go after, I can adjust my mindset to offset anything they could grasp onto."

Rosa slowly shook her head.

Tony was silent.

Bill observed the altercation with great interest.

Rosa then smiled kindly. "Mary, you don't have to go through the stress of court proceedings. Tony is offering you a clean-cut way to end this problem for good. Nobody has to get hurt if you don't want it that way. There's all kinds of ways to handle this little problem."

"Little?" I repeated defensively.

Tony spoke up in a whisper. "It's little for our friend. That's what Rosa meant. We know it's no little matter to you. That's why we care so much. That's why we want to help you end it." He looked me in the eye. "Nobody has to know what transpired. One day, out of the blue, you'll get your book contracts back in the mail and all rights will again belong to you. Nobody will be the wiser. It can be that easy."

I eyed him back. "I'll be the wiser. I'll know. I don't solve my problems with violence or by making threats. Making an offer that can't be refused is still making a threat. I don't operate that way. I'll take my chances with the law. If my battleground ends up being a courtroom. . .then so be it."

"Won't you even take a little time to consider it?" Rosa pleaded.

"There's nothing to consider." I looked over to Tony. "Tony, I appreciate you giving up this favor that's owed you. I appreciate you wanting to call it in for me, but I just can't do it."

He put his hands up. "It's your call. I understand."

Two days later when our friends were getting in their car to leave, Tony looked me in the eye. "Do any thinking about that offer?"

I smiled. I shook my head.

"It's still on the table if you change your mind."

I kissed him. "I love you guys. Have a safe trip back."

In January of 1992, when the manuscript for my journal was all set to send to my publisher, I happened to be talking on the phone to our attorney in Virginia. I'd casually mentioned a few things I'd written in the soon-to-be-published journal about our publishing problems and he became concerned. He wanted to review every sentence and word I'd written about the issue.

"How come I can't write about it?" I asked.

"Because you may have said some things they can use

against you. Nothing's been proven yet, so you have to be careful what you say."

"Like what, for instance?"

"Like, for instance, you can't say anything that may make them sound guilty before the case is tried in court. The court decides who's guilty."

I was silent.

"Mary? You understand what I said?"

"Yeah. I guess that means I shouldn't have called them crooks then, huh."

"You called them *crooks* in your *manuscript*?"

"Guess I can't do that, can I."

"No you can't do that!"

"Uh-oh. Well. . .maybe I shouldn't have also written about the mafia hit that was offered to me either."

"WHAT!"

Oops.

"Talk to me, Mary. Tell me about this hit thing."

John Hart, attorney-at-law, listened intently while I explained how I'd been offered the favor that would end my problems.

"You can't publish that!"

"Why? It happened. This journal is about what happens in my day-to-day life."

"Getting an offer from a friend of a hit man is *not* day-to-day stuff in one's life! You haven't thought this out."

"What do you mean?"

"Look. What if that publisher had had a bad accident or a major mishap with his house or warehouse. Who do you think would be the first person they'd come looking for if you printed that offer in your book?"

"That's silly, John. I also wrote how I turned it down."

I heard a deep sigh. "That won't matter one bit. You would still be the first suspect."

"Suspect?"

"Mary. . .just send me that manuscript. OVERNIGHT!"

So now, just when I needed to get the manuscript to the publisher, I had to delay that by first sending it off to my attorney so he could redline it. This was a delay we couldn't afford, yet had to be done.

When the journal was published, much of what I'd written had been deleted by our attorney. I guess Rosa was right. I'm too honest. My innocence (or ignorance) could very well get me in a lot of trouble.

*Soul Sounds* was released in March of 1992. Some of the publishing problems were left in. Consequently, the reading public learned of the situation and three months following publication, I received a letter from a Native American man. He was a Dog Soldier. He said he loved me and had heard about my problems. He offered to "take care" of this publisher for me. He made it clear what his intent was. He, like our friends, was offering to solve my problem in an unconventional, but final, manner. This native man said that white law was no good. He assured me that the only way to get real justice was to handle things through his Dog Soldiers.

I sat for a long while with his letter in my hand. It seemed that I had friends who wouldn't hesitate to "fire" for me. I was incredulous that another offer had come to me. It appeared that there were those who loved me with a deadly kind of love. I couldn't imagine anyone wanting to solve my problems by erasing the cause, especially when the cause is a living person.

I wrote a carefully-worded response to this man. I didn't want to offend him or seem as though I'd rejected his gift, yet I think I managed to discourage him in the most gentle manner I knew to use.

The following month I met with a biker. We'd prearranged a meeting in the lounge at the Fossil Inn in Florissant which was only a mile south of my house.

I was there before him. When he strode in, I saw a large man in studded black leather. I also saw his gentle heart.

I stood.

We hugged.

He held me at arm's length and looked into my eyes. "You sure are a lot prettier in person," he whispered.

I blushed and wondered if that meant my book photos were ugly or if he was just flattering me.

We sat at the small, round cocktail table.

After chatting over generalities for a bit, he got to his point of the meeting.

"I'm gonna Bull Dog for you."

"You're gonna what?"

He smiled wide. "I'm gonna take care of your problem."

"What problem?"

"That crud publisher. . .he won't be making any more trouble for you."

My heart nearly stopped with the implication. I couldn't believe this was happening a third time. "You can't do that."

"Little Lady, I can do anything I want. And I do!"

I had the feeling that nobody told him what he could and couldn't do. His next words confirmed it.

"*Nobody* tells me I *can't* do something!"

I looked him in the eye. "I just did. I'm telling you that you can't do that."

His unexpected wide grin surprised me. That was the last response I thought would be forthcoming.

"What's so funny?" I asked.

He looked about and lowered his voice. "I just felt like you was No-Eyes scoldin' me. It gave me a chill. It felt good."

I smiled back. The shaky incident was on terra firma again. "Then listen to her. Do you think she'd let you do that for her? Do you think your way would be *her* way to solve things?"

He sighed and looked down at the tabletop. "No, ma'am."

I rested my hand on his arm.

He looked over at it.

I whispered. "I can see how No-Eyes has affected your life. . .within you."

He interrupted. "It was you who affected my life."

"Regardless, I understand your anger over my troubles. A lot of people are outraged over it too. But, in keeping with what No-Eyes taught, we all have to follow the spiritual manner of solving our problems."

He raised his hand and looked me in the eye.

I continued. "You would honor No-Eyes and respect my wishes if you just forgot about this whole thing. The thought of you wanting to help me is a beautiful gift all by itself. I accept that thought and desire to help me. I accept your gift of thought. It's a gift of support that warms my heart. It has served the beautiful purpose of showing that folks are behind me. I don't need more. More would only tarnish the gift you've already given me. Please forget about doing anything more."

Silence.

"Please?"

He reluctantly nodded.

I brightened. "You'll stick to your word?"

"For you. For you I'll keep my word."

"Thank you. You've made me very happy."

He stood.

I followed suit.

We hugged again and he lifted my chin with a calloused finger.

"You're some lady." And he left.

I sat back down. The roar of his Harley rumbled through the Inn. I listened to the sound as it travelled further and further away. Mixed feelings swirled within me. The biker had come with a violent offer and, although it'd been rejected, he'd left carrying a warmed heart that a special promise had filled. . .he'd just exchanged one favor for another kind.

We were both appeased.


And so these three hit offers caused me a great deal of contemplation. I understood the love behind them. I understood the outrage over injustices one sees being done to a friend or a loved one. I understood the need to want to help. Yet the manner of solution remains an enigma to me. How can it be that the love and the solution can exist within one heart. . .simultaneously?

And so I could do nothing but accept the fact that I had unknown friends out there who loved me and cared enough to want to offer their friendly fire on my behalf. It was not an especially comforting thought, yet because it proved to be fact, it was one I had to accept with all the grace I could muster toward it. I couldn't change the fact that deadly love existed. . .I could only change some of the endings.

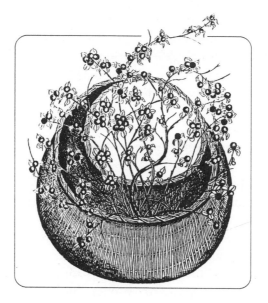

# DUELING MINDS

On Friday, March 20th, I had my last telephone conversation with my publisher, Bob Friedman, before we would see him in Norfolk a few days later. His parting words to me were "Have a safe trip and bring Snowmaker with you."

I thought that was funny. "You don't really want me to bring Snowmaker with me, do you?"

He chuckled. "Yeah, I do. Bill's always telling me about all that snow you get, it'd be nice to see a little here."

I smiled at the thought. "Okay, Bob, I'll see what I can do."

Saturday was a hectic day for the entire family. Bill and I and the three girls were packing. The five of us were making the cross-country drive to Virginia Beach where we had hotel reservations. This was not a journey-of-choice. It was a mandatory trip for Bill and me. We had to give our depositions to our opponents' attorneys. And because it'd been many years since the whole family went anywhere together, we decided to try and make it a semi-vacation for the family. It's funny, we used to chuckle when tourists would come to our area and we'd hear them comment that these were the first mountains they'd ever seen. What? Never seen a mountain before? Where have you been all your life? Yet now, now we were taking our girls to *see* an ocean—for the first time. Seagulls. Real sand. Ocean waves. Seashells. Oh, how excited they were. They were so excited that going to bed that night proved to be a real silly idea. We were in the van by 3:00 A.M. Sunday morning. Now that we were on our way, they dozed while dad drove. They dozed until the brilliant orange daybreak greeted them for their wakeup call. Yeah! We're gonna see an ocean!

The journey took us three days. The girls took turns spelling the driver. On Tuesday, the twenty-fourth, when we were checking in at the Virginia Beach Days Inn, the clerk looked out the front windows. His eyes widened. His mouth fell. "Will you look at that! Snow!" We looked. We smiled. "Yeah. That's snow alright." Guess our Colorado Snowmaker fella hitched a ride on our back bumper. Later, I was told that folks in Virginia Beach who knew I was coming to town said, "It's snowing! Mary Summer Rain must've arrived." Of course, we didn't really bring the snow with us—at least I don't think we did.

After we checked in, the clerk handed us a message. John Nelson, one of the other authors participating in the lawsuit, wanted us to call him. Bill called after we settled in. John wanted to know if he and his lady friend could come up to our room to discuss things. That was fine with us.

We talked for a few hours. He'd already given his deposition. It appeared that, during it, he had difficulty containing his anger and frustrations. He'd let the opposition's attorneys push his buttons; therefore, they kept calling him back. Out of all John had said, I got the message to remain unflustered while being deposed. . .no matter what they said, inferred or tried to claim. Well yeah, I could do that. No problem. I knew this was going to be a mental duel—one between a little mountain woman and hot shot Kansas City and Norfolk attorneys. Yeah, I could stay calm. I could do that. In fact, I was looking forward to facing them across the battlefield of their polished oak table. Yeah. Shift to Warrior Mode. No sweat.

After John and his lady left, we had a few hours of free time before we were scheduled to have dinner with the Hampton Roads crew. We went out on the beach. It was cold, but Aimee and Sarah donned shorts and treated their legs to the first-time-ever feel of ocean waves. They were having the time of their lives. Jenny, on the other hand, being the more conservative of the three, walked the beach in shoes and winter jacket. For her, just being there and seeing all that water was a thrill—not to mention how much fun she had feeding the gangs of gulls. I imagine the old salts who live locally think the gulls are nothing more than pests to be tolerated, yet for mountain folk, they and the ocean were part and parcel of the same wonder.

Bill, too, loved the ocean. This was not his first time at one. He'd been stationed in Monterey many years ago and I'd visited him there. And, a few years before this current trip, he and I had journeyed out to visit our Norfolk publisher. Bill loved the ocean. He had a strong affinity with it, and I too always felt drawn to the coast of Maine where breakers resoundingly crashed on rocky shores. I can't explain this draw I've always had for the Maine coast. Perhaps I'll never find out unless I journey there one day.

Playtime over, we got ready for dinner. Ah, seafood. Real seafood. We loved it and were anxious to be on our way. The restaurant was wonderful, not only because of its sumptuous fare, but also for its pier location and maritime atmosphere. Everything about the dinner was perfect—the company we were in made it so. Each and every person at Hampton Roads was warm and friendly. They made us feel like family and, after dinner, we brought them into our own family by sharing Aimee's birthday celebration. This day had marked her twentieth birthday and I'd brought along a few presents for her to open at the dinner table. Afterward, we took some group pictures and then shared goodbyes, for Bill and I were due at our attorneys' office at 9:00 P.M. for our pre-deposition briefing.

We dropped the girls back at the hotel and went to meet our attorneys, John Hart and Jack Keller. When we arrived, we were ushered into the conference room. General instructional ground rules for the deposition process were given. Mr. Hart outlined the sequence of questioning that the other attorneys followed with the previous authors who'd already been deposed. We were the last ones. We had some questions that were answered. I think our attorneys felt we were strong clients until. . .

"They're going to bring No-Eyes into this," John said.

"Why? What's she got to do with illegal dealings?" I responded.

"She's what your books are about."

"So?" I sighed. "What does the subject matter of my books—or, for that matter, any of the authors' books—have to do with anything?"

Then John sighed. "Subject matter and what someone says (or writes) can be used to various ends. The big question they've asked each of the authors so far is 'What is New Age?'"

Now it was perfectly clear. They were going to try to make me look like a nutty fruitcake.

"So what did the other authors answer to that question?" I asked.

"Everyone said something different. Some were vague while others mentioned crystals and fortune telling."

I thought that whoever mentioned those things had dug their own grave. "Well, I have my own answer to that question. That one doesn't bother me. What bothers me is their ploy to discredit No-Eyes or make her sound like a looney." I pointed to the set of my books on the conference table. "Those are not cookbooks. They. . .they represent a very special person. And. . .and she was taken—stolen—from me." Tears formed in my eyes.

John and Jack looked at one another.

Their strong client was folding.

"I'm sorry," I apologized. "I'm sorry, but this whole mess has been a big strain on me. Those books are not paper and ink—they're someone's flesh and blood."

"Well," John began, "we understand that. We understand what they mean to you, but the other attorneys see them for their content. They'll still bring No-Eyes into it."

"Well, fine! Let them!"

Mr. Hart then reviewed several points in the filed complaint that I needed to remember. My head spun with the various figures and related claims. Why'd I have to know all that precise legal stuff? Isn't that why I had attorneys? I wrote down notes to study and memorize for the deposition in the morning. It seemed like Greek to me.

As we concluded the conference I had a final question for our attorneys.

"Will we be required to walk through a metal detector?"

Odd question.

The two men exchanged glances.

"No," John Hart said. "Why?"

I pointed to my purse. "Because I carry a gun. I don't go anywhere without my little .380 9mm."

John swallowed hard.

Jack Keller smiled coolly. "My wife carries a gun, too. Women need protection these days. You'll be okay. Nobody's going to check for that."

I patted my purse. I smiled. "Good."

When we returned to the hotel, the girls were out on the balcony. Heavy blankets were wrapped around them. They were listening to the ocean surf.

I took out my notes and began to study them. I was tired. The more I read them over, the more confused I became. To heck with this, I decided. And I made my own little cheat sheet. I'd keep it in my lap during the deposition and just nonchalantly look down at it when needed.

With that problem solved, I got ready for bed. The others were already tucked in. I closed my eyes and mentally prepared for battle. *I'm going to be strong tomorrow. . .those hot shots won't intimidate me. . .I can play their little game too. . .I'm going to be strong.* And the litany was repeated like a mantra until the sound of waves lulled me into a deep sleep. I slept like a baby until 4:00 A.M. when my churning stomach slammed reality in my face. Every nerve in my body was electrified. Shakily, I crawled out of bed and went into the bathroom. Hands on the counter to steady myself, I looked into the mirror.

The reflection was a stranger.

The stranger was telepathic.

"Why are you doing this to No-Eyes?" it demanded to know of me. "I thought you loved her. Haven't you hurt her enough by letting her get away from you? You've failed her once, now you're going to have her name muddied. What's the matter with you? Go home! NOW! Go pack and go home! You don't have to hurt her more than you already have. You don't have to go through with this. *Save* her from humiliation! Go home! Go *home!* NOW!"

I felt so sick. Really sick. I sat on the edge of the tub and bent my head to my knees. I began to cry. To sob. . .hard.

"Oh my No-Eyes. Oh, my sweet No-Eyes. I'm so sorry I couldn't hold onto you. I'm so sorry I failed to protect you. You're gone and now I'm about to drag you through the mud. Oh. . .GOD!"

As I cried my eyes out and held my stomach, I remembered Tony's words. "Those attorneys are gonna chew you up and spit you out. . .*spit you out.* They're gonna make you look like a crazy person. . .*crazy person.* You don't have an attorney's mind. . .*mind.* They'll drag No-Eyes through the mud. . .*No-Eyes through the mud.*"

I sobbed harder. Louder.

I moaned and rocked back and forth.

"I love you, No-Eyes. Okay, I won't do this to you. I won't hurt you anymore. I'll protect your honor. I won't go through with this. We'll go home. Yeah. We'll go home right now."

Bill came into the bathroom. Kneeling down beside me, he held me. "Honey, you sick? What's wrong?" he asked, brushing back the hair from my face.

"I can't do this."

"Can't do what?"

"The deposition!" I sobbed. "I'm not doing it."

"You have to. Honey, we have to go through with it."

I screamed at him. "No. . .we. . .don't! *We* don't have to do *anything!* We. . .are. . .going. . .*home!*"

By this time, the girls were up. When I stormed out of the bathroom and began gathering our belongings to pack, Bill gently took my arm.

"Honey, sit down."

I yanked my arm out of his grip. "Don't patronize me! I

don't even know what I'm doing here. I belong up in the mountains. What am I doing with slick city attorneys all fancied up in their prim little Brooks Brothers suits anyway? I'm going back to the real world. We have to pack!"

Sarah asked, "Why, mom?"

"Why? Because we're not doing the deposition, that's why."

"But you have to, mom."

I flared at her. "Don't *tell* me what I *have* to do! You—*none* of you—understand. You just don't get it! I can't *hurt* her anymore!" I then sat on the end of the bed and began sobbing my heart out again. I could not stop. I mumbled words to No-Eyes and nothing existed but me sitting there talking and apologizing to her.

The family was scared. They'd never seen me like that. I hadn't ever seen me like that. I was scaring myself. One thing was certain though—we were going home. We were going home NOW!

I heard Bill speaking with someone on the phone.

Suddenly it was in my lap.

"Bob wants to talk to you," he softly said.

"Why'd you wake him up? We're going home."

"I wanted to see if Katie could give you something. She's a doctor and can help you."

"I don't need a doctor. I need to go back to Colorado. I need to go back into the woods where things are real."

He held the receiver out before me. "Please? Please talk to Bob?"

I grabbed the damn thing just to shut him up. "Bob," I cried, "I can't do this. They're gonna try an' make her look bad. I can't do this to her. I'm going home."

"Mary," came the soft voice, "you have to go through with this. You have to do it for No-Eyes."

"No. It's only going to hurt her more. I can't hurt her any more."

"No. It won't hurt her, Mary. You have to fight for her."

"I'd do anything for her. . .but. . .oh God, Bob. . .they've *had* her for so *long!*"

"Now's your chance to take her back. It's the only way. It's the only way to get her back. If you go home without going through with this deposition, they'll strike you from the suit and you'll never get her back. Katie wants to talk to you."

Katie's voice was calm. "Mary?"

"What."

"Mary, you're having a panic attack."

Oh. Right.

"Now listen to me," she said. "You can get through this. I know you can."

"You don't understand," I cried.

"Yes I do. Now I want you to go into the bathroom and take a nice hot bath."

Silence. Bath? *Bath*? And she was a *doctor*?

"Mary?"

Silence.

"Mary?"

"I'm here."

"Did you hear me?"

"I heard."

"Will you do that for me?"

"It's not going to help. I need to go home."

"Will you take that hot bath first?"

I said I would just to get her off my case.

Bill took the phone from me. In a daze I shuffled into the bathroom and ran the shower. I took hot showers, not baths.

I stood under the hot water for a long while. For a long while I just stood there like a wet mannequin. Then, slowly, ever so slowly, I began moving. The hair got shampooed. It felt wonderful. Something was draining from me and the stream of water was washing it away. Vigorously I towel-dried then wrapped my hair. When I wiped the mirror clear of steam, I looked into it.

The stranger was gone.

The eyes of a warrior looked back at me. And I smiled into them. "You *have* to fight for her. You *have* to do battle to get her back." The warrior was calm. Sure. Determined.

With the towel wrapped around me, I entered the room.

My poor family. They were like frozen statues—so expectant were they.

Without saying a word, I went to the suitcase and pulled

out my slip. Not the "going home" jeans, but my "Wednesday-go-to-deposition" clothes.

Everyone sighed and smiled. They rushed over to me and crushed me with hugs.

"We knew you'd do it, mom!"

"For No-Eyes," I said. "For No-Eyes."

Relieved, they went out on the balcony to feed the gulls.

I returned to the bathroom to dress and attempt major repair work on my red and swollen eyes. While trying to perform this make-up miracle, I heard Bill on the phone. Shortly thereafter, the phone rang.

"Was that Bob?" I asked, peeking around the bathroom door.

"No. That was John Hart calling back."

"Oh?"

"I called him while you were in the shower. I told him about your panic attack and concern for No-Eyes. He called the other attorneys. They're not going to bring her into this."

I was floored. "He didn't have to make a deal, did he?"

"He didn't say. Maybe they thought the only way to get our depositions was to agree to lay off No-Eyes. I don't really know."

"Well. . .I'm okay now. That's still good news, though."

As I was drying the last of my hair, I heard Bob and Katie come in. When I greeted them, Katie was genuinely happy to see me. She smiled wide and exclaimed, "And she's even got make-up on!" She seemed surprised I'd managed that feat. It made me wonder if people just over a panic attack didn't usually care about such trivialities as their appearance. We hugged. We hugged and I felt bad for my previous thoughts of her being a bad doctor. . .she was a damned good one. . .she knew her stuff.

We talked a little. She and Bob had stopped by to offer some moral support, yet I found that I was still too sensitive to even mention No-Eyes' name, for tears found their way out of my eyes when I voiced it. I quickly recovered. "Guess we won't talk about her right now." Everyone understood.

Then it was time to go.

Jenny and Aimee had planned to do a little shopping while we were gone. Sarah wanted to come with us. Bob and Katie accompanied us down to the lobby and they wished us luck.

The ride from Virginia Beach into the heart of Norfolk was not enjoyable. I had to stop twice. The emotionally-charged morning had left my system upset. Thankfully, Bill had brought along some great medicine that fixed me up. My body may have had some negative effects from the morning's duel with myself, but my mind was right on target. I was heading toward the battleground. I was prepared to fight for No-Eyes. I could feel the strength within me and it felt wonderful.

We found the office building without any problem. When we rode the elevator up to the attorneys' office complex, we watched the doors open onto a plush reception area. We were seated and offered something to drink. We declined. Shortly thereafter, our attorneys arrived. Bill shook hands with them. I gave each a hug. Jack seemed confident. John's shirt was damp.

"I'm okay now," I reassured him. "Thanks for your special efforts this morning. I appreciate it."

He smiled.

I think John Hart was a bit nervous. He knew I'd had a severe emotional episode that morning that may have left me in a less-than-stable state. He knew I'd been really upset with the other attorneys. He knew I'd strongly react if they brought up the subject of No-Eyes. And he knew I was going in there with a gun.

"They're ready for us," he finally said.

Bill and Sarah settled themselves in the reception area while I, accompanied by our two attorneys, walked onto the battleground at exactly 9:15 in the morning.

I'm honor-bound to not reveal any precise details of the deposition proceedings; therefore, we'll shift to generalities.

When we broke for lunch and the five of us were taking a well-deserved breather, Jack Keller said that I was doing great in there. John Hart agreed and said, "They like you."

While I nibbled some lunch, I wondered about John's statement. What did it mean when the opposition's attorneys "liked you"? Did that mean you were easy and could be smoothly manipulated? Or did it mean that you made an honorable opponent for them? Or did it mean what he said—that they just plain liked me for me? Well, I never did ask for a clarification. It really didn't seem to matter all that much to me. And, by now, I could tell that my attorneys had no more anxiety about me or. . .my purse.

After the lunch break, the battle waged on until 5:30 P.M. The ordeal lasted seven hours. I shook the two opposing attorneys' hands and smiled at them. They smiled back. And as I was leaving the room, one whispered to the other, "We forgot to ask her the New Age question."

"Eh, let it go," said the other.

I smiled again as I walked out the door. I wish they had asked me that one, for I had two responses ready. One was a smart-mouth answer and the other was the real one. What does New Age mean? New Age is an Age that's New, like the Ice Age was an Age of Ice or the Iron Age was the Age of Iron. That was, obviously, the smart-mouth answer. My real one was to be: New Age is the gentle blend of physics and spiritual-ity—science meets religion.

I'd found that, after a short while into the confrontation with the two opposition attorneys, I was actually enjoying the duel. They grinned the first time I'd called them "sir." I don't believe they expected to be addressed in a respectful manner. I smiled at them quite a bit. Genuine smiles. After all, my beef was not with these two men, it was with their clients. I answered questions with questions which, I was strongly informed, was a no-no for the deponent. Yet I persisted with the response— whenever I thought it was required. I could not be forced or intimidated by raised voices into responding to a particular question I wanted re-worded. They refused to re-word it and, eventually, they dropped the question altogether—going in circles wasted time, I guess. No-Eyes had made me an expert in verbal circle dances. It finally came in handy. I was so "into" the mental play that I was actually disappointed when it was concluded. By the time Bill and I switched places in the reception area, I was on a mental high. I sat with Sarah while our attorneys accompanied Bill onto the battlefield at 5:45 P.M. After a time, we heard laughter coming from the room. Sarah and I looked at one another, then grinned. How was Bill amusing them? The incident never made it into the transcript. The humor was an off-the-record comment Bill's persistent response had elicited from one of the opposition's attorneys.

Mr. Hart, Mr. Keller and Bill came out of the conference room at 7:15. They were smiling.

It was over. *Now* we could go home.

We drove back to the hotel and shared our day with the girls. They expressed their happiness over how it had all worked out. Then we discussed our plans. We were supposed to leave for home the following morning, yet decided to stay over one more day. It had been a harrowing time for all of us and, now that the depositions were behind us, we wanted to salvage some portion of the trip by having the girls see a few sights—one day set aside for relaxation wasn't a bad idea.

So, on Thursday, we played tourist and spent time on the beach. Though it was still very cold and sometimes rainy, we managed to ignore both. We were glad we'd stayed over.

Bright and early—before dawn—we were driving out of Virginia Beach and heading home. With Sarah and Aimee taking turns at the wheel, we made it home in two days. There's no fooling around when you're heading home.

But there's one more mental duel we had participated in. This was not within one's own mind, as mine had been. Neither was this with an attorney. This duel came quite unexpectedly and occurred without any of us realizing it was taking place. It was a "fool-you" duel.

We were passing through Kentucky. Bill was driving. Jenny enjoyed following the city signs as we passed them and she'd announce them to me. I had the map and played navigator. When she called out a town name, I suddenly lost my place. I asked her to repeat it. She did. Finally I found the town on the map.

My scalp crawled.

"You sure, Jen?"

"Yeah." And she spelled it just before announcing another upcoming town sign.

I quickly checked the map for that one. She was right. That gave me a cold chill.

"Ah-h-h. . .does anyone remember going through Lexington?" I asked.

"Right, mom," Sarah joked.

Bill laughed. "Is that a trick question?"

I frowned then. "I don't know, is it?"

Sarah responded. "You tell us. We don't know what you're talking about."

"Hey!" I sparked, "what's so complicated? I just want to know if anyone recalls going through Lexington? No biggie, just answer me."

Aimee thought she was being cute. "Yeah, I remember. . ."

Relief.

". . .on the way *out* here!" she finished.

I didn't want cute. I wanted a straight answer.

Jenny called out another town. I checked. I was silent for awhile. Then, "Has anyone been keeping track of the time? When was the last time someone looked at their watch?"

No one had bothered about the time.

Sarah became more interested. "Mom? Is this some new game?"

My tone was unmistakable. "I'm serious. I want to know if anyone recalls going through Lexington?"

They looked at one another as if poor ole mom had finally gone over the edge.

Aimee sounded concerned. "Well no, mom. We haven't gotten that far yet."

Bill glanced over at me. "There a problem, honey?"

I met his eyes. "Is that right? We haven't gone that far yet?"

He grinned. "Sounds like the navigator lost her place."

I stared at him. My voice was low. "Sounds more like this whole van lost its place. We are a couple of hours *past* Lexington."

No one breathed.

I continued. "This whole van has lost time. We are missing a whole *block* of time."

Everyone was silent.

Then Sarah found her voice. "Nahhh."

"That can't be," Aimee added.

Jenny smiled. "Really?"

"Really?" Bill echoed.

"Really."

And after everyone had to personally check the map for

themselves, it was unanimously agreed on that we were far past Lexington while everyone swore we were nowhere near it yet.

Mind games.

"So where *were* we?" Sarah wondered aloud.

Nobody had an answer.

Jenny sighed. "Oh no, not *Them* again."

Aimee was confused. "How'd they do that in daylight? Did the van and us just disappear off the road? Wouldn't other drivers kinda notice a little trick like that? And did we just reappear hours and miles ahead? I don't get this."

Who really could? I tried an answer. "Visual hologram trickery and psychological manipulation along with mass telepathic hypnosis. Remember my couch experience? How'd they come for me that night without Magic being the wiser? We can't begin to explain or figure these things out without having a basic understanding of such advanced methods."

For a long while, none of us spoke. We were each deep in the wondering depths of our own churning and straining minds. What's curiously interesting to me personally is the fact that no one mentioned the experience again. Ever.

It was as though it never happened. Yet. . .considering our experience with routine encounters at Grand Central Station, is it really any wonder why *this* one should be marked as being any more remarkable than any of the others? Had we, by way of our family's experiential history, become so immune to these encounters that we now perceive them as the norm? Could be. Could be, for I had no other explanation.

As time passed, our little vacation to Virginia Beach became jokingly known as The Trip To Hell. I think it was Aimee that started saying it. And, with hindsight, it was indeed apropos. Oh yes, for sure Virginia Beach is a beautiful place to visit and live, but the way we had to ignore the cold and rain put a bit of a serious damper on the girls' first ocean experience. The highly-charged incident of my frightening panic attack put everyone around me through a type of hellish experience that scared the daylights out of them. Me too, for that matter. And our missing miles and time only put the frosting on the cake. It was a trip packed full of new experiences for all of us. . .experiences none of us would willingly choose to have again.

# FAIREST OF THE FAIR

Somewhere around the last part of February and the first of March, I'd received a letter from a gentleman by the name of Shanti Toll. Shanti was one of the owners of a little shop called Celebration that was located in a white frame house in Old Colorado City. Celebration was well-known as "the" metaphysical source to browse through for everything from books to incense to art prints of angels.

Twice a year, spring and fall, Shanti hosted a large metaphysical fair that was held in a Colorado Springs auditorium. This fair was the subject of Shanti's correspondence. He was inquiring about my interest in making a special appearance and participating in the three-day event. I believe he knew of my reluctance to make public appearances because he'd cleverly— yet subtly—worded his invitation in a manner that touched my heartstrings. He gently referred to the large readership I had in the area and, wouldn't it be wonderful to connect with them. Although I doubt he meant it, I interpreted his phrasing like this: "You have a lot of fans around here who've bought a lot of your books—you owe them a gesture of appreciation!" Does that sound like what Catholics call an "over-scrupulous conscience?" Guilt. Guilt pressed on my shoulders. Well, it had been quite a few years since I'd done a book signing (back when *Phoenix Rising* was released) and, if the reality of it be known, I did love doing them. As long as I didn't have to give a public speech, I loved meeting my readers. Touching with them by way of holding their hands or getting up and giving them hugs came so natural to me because I truly cared about them. It wasn't as simple as an expression of an author's appreciation for her/his readers; it went far, far deeper than that. It was more like—I love you because you've cherished No-Eyes.

Bill and I discussed Shanti's invitation. The event was scheduled to take place after our depositions were over. We saw no reason to decline. Bill then called Hampton Roads to discuss it with Bob and, before I knew it, preparations were in the making. Bill got in touch with Shanti, who was very glad to hear we'd be there. When we received the auditorium layout and saw the space we were tentatively scheduled to occupy, we knew there was a problem with it. The line would either block the flow of traffic or it would hide many other booths. We couldn't have either. Bill immediately contacted Shanti, who circumvented the problem by placing us at one end of the entry hall which gave us a lot of space—too much space.

Within the blink of an owl's eye, a great idea came to me. We could invite Carole Bourdo to be there too! Oh, I loved it. So when Bill called Carole, she liked the idea a lot. Only problem for her was that she couldn't be there the final day; she'd been scheduled to be elsewhere on Easter.

Our next step was to visit the auditorium so we could plan out how we'd set everything up. Bill is always insistent that people can't get around behind me. We handled this issue by planning to utilize each of the balcony stairway landings as the places where we'd set up our tables—Carole on one landing, and me across from her on the other one. Lauri, Carole's daughter, had accompanied us and she liked the idea too. Lauri worked out the entire setup of her mom's artwork display. She'd done this preliminary work for countless art shows. She knew her stuff.

We made the event a family affair. Aimee was scheduled to read to the children from *Mountains, Meadows and Moonbeams.* Jenny and Sarah were my assistants. Robin and Aimee's friend, Martha, handled book sales. Our friend, Frank Gonzalez, and Lauri's friend, Don Carey, worked security. Security? How silly. But Bill and Lauri insisted, especially since her friend worked with the federal marshals. And Bill, of course, had the important job of visiting with those who came to see us. Visiting. Talking and laughing. Answering questions and sometimes counselling. Yes, very important work. And how he loves it!

The first day of the fair was Friday, April 17th. We were all excited. Native American music was playing softly in the background of our area and I burned cedar incense on the stair beside me. The atmosphere was set. When I looked up from lighting the cedar, a smiling face was there looking back at me. Behind that face were others—one behind another—all the way down the hall. The line had formed without me even seeing it manifest. Later I was told that folks stood in line for three hours. I felt bad about that because it was all my fault that they had to wait so long. I talk to people. I get up and give them long hugs when I feel they want or need one. Sometimes they'll ask for a hug or ask if Bill can take their picture with me. I don't like having my picture taken, but I never decline a request. All this extra attention to people takes time, yet they willingly wait their turn because they know I'll give them all the time they need too. Because of this long wait for people to stand in line, I insist that no elder, no mother carrying an infant, and no handicapped person be forced to endure the wait. These are brought forward by my assistants and I visit with them first. People's children can sit on my lap while I sign their parent's book.

I had some surprises during the fair's three days. Some women I hugged ended up clutching me and sobbing their eyes out. I closed my eyes and tried to soothe them. One woman later wrote me to explain how her day-long migraine had vanished after we hugged. People were so patient and understanding. The atmosphere was one of gaiety and yet, at other times, it was so weighted it felt sacred.

Gifts too, surprised me. Hand-beaded medicine bags, to flowers, to a basket of Pepsi.

Books! People brought bags of books with them. I signed fourteen for one woman. Do you know how difficult it is to concentrate on writing fourteen different names when someone's talking to you and asking questions? No simple feat. I'm still not sure I got those names right.

I was embarrassed when Bill came up to me for the lunch breaks. I'd look up at the waiting faces and want to keep going. But he insists I get at least a few minutes rest and eat something for energy. I keep telling him that the people themselves give me all the energy I need, but he doesn't quite buy that. So I apologize to the next person in line and leave the table for a short spell.

Shanti had provided us with our own breakroom. It was a backstage dressing room. To get there, though, I had to walk the entire length of the packed auditorium that was lined with booths and a full complement of visitors. Well, that was fine, but Mr. Carey had to stride before me to watch out and lead the way. He did a great job—nobody wanted to tangle with Mr. Carey.

Throughout the three days, everyone had a fun time. On the last day, though, I missed Carole's presence. She's such a gracious and gregarious individual and I love her so much. Her absence was deeply felt that last day. I'd missed her.

In the fair's final hour, when people were packing up their booths and most of the visitors had left, a burly biker came up and tightly hugged me. I was startled. I glanced around for Bill and our security men—they were all busy going back and forth to the van. Perfect. Perfect chance for someone to get to me. Ah, but this particular young man had his soul shining through those eyes of his. This was no threat. This was unconditional love. This was honor. Respect.

And I hugged back.

That evening we gathered at the house and talked about each of our experiences throughout the fair. Everyone had done a great job and was ready to do it again. And again.

Before I drifted off to sleep that night, I too had thoughts that kept returning again and again. I'd recall the special expression someone had, or someone's heartfelt words. I'd visualize a drawing a child made for me, or the special hug someone needed. Such love filled the space at the end of that hall. People had commented on feeling the comfort and peace that permeated our area. Thinking on that as I lay in bed, I smiled. Surely those people had to know why they felt what they did. It wasn't me. It wasn't Carole. *We* weren't the fairest of the fair. . .all those loving *people* were!

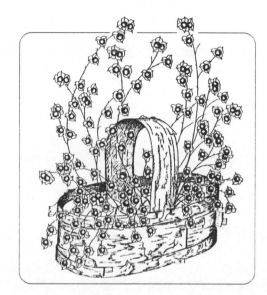

# LOOKING FOR GOODHEART

The germinating seeds of this story began back in 1991. It's another major life situation of ours that was edited out of the *Soul Sounds* book at the last moment when I'd been checking the final proof pages of the text. We were forced to pull the incidents because of the possibility of a lawsuit against my publisher if the story was published. Needless to say, because the events caused us such deep heartache, I passionately objected to the eleventh-hour change in the book. How was it, I wondered, that I seemed to be prevented from writing about the causes of our deepest pains? How was it that so much had to be hidden from our life in deference to the fragile sensitivities and egos of the pain-bringers? Yet, forever being one to avoid conflict, I combed the typeset pages and deleted all reference to those involved in the incidents and then had to revise for continuity. Those who know me can imagine the dark mood this activity brought upon me. Anger and hurt. The injustice of it. The extra work involved for me and the typesetter at Hampton Roads, and the added time delay in getting the book out on time all added to my feelings of defeat. This defeat was not related to a battle-type situation, but rather was the feeling of not being free to write honestly of the events in our lives—the fact that major portions of our story were prevented from being told.

Eventually, both Bill and I allowed Acceptance to blanket the situation and we continued on with our lives. We held no grudges or animosity toward anyone. It all would've been forgotten if it hadn't been for the far-reaching ramifications the deleted events had on our lives. Little did we know then how deeply they would intrude into our future. . .to the point of wreaking total destruction.

So then, because the events of 1991 have so fiercely ripped the fabric of our lives for the next three and a half years, I cannot continue in honesty without going back and exposing the event that cast down a black shadow over our lives for so long.

Around 1987 I began corresponding with a young woman by the name of *Vickie. She lived in a southern state and we became close through the years. In 1991, Bill began having long talks with her over the telephone. She'd been having some problems in her life and with spiritual direction. Bill seemed to be able to assist her in many ways. Through inner guidance she'd experienced a strong pull toward Colorado and was seriously planning on relocating here. She'd felt her purpose was to be directly involved with us in some capacity. This prompting precipitated a trip out to see us in May. We were excited to finally meet our long-distance friend, especially since we'd also found out that she'd been with us in a previous lifetime as Bill's wife when I was She-Who-Sees.

Vickie was very interested in seeing some of Colorado. We decided the perfect opportunity would be to take her with us on a journey to the Marble area to see the property we were drawn to. Bill, Vickie and I took off early in the morning for the trip (she had to be deleted out of this Marble journey in *Soul Sounds*).

Driving along the Crystal River Valley toward Marble, we neared the Redstone area and a beautiful floating mist descended softly over the region. The mist had the feeling of angel wings. It affected the three of us in a manner that was beautiful and profound. So profound that Bill had to pull off the road to let it wrap us in the deep love it was emitting. Vickie and I got out of the car and stood in awe of the permeating essence that touched each of us. We gazed up at the high pine-covered ridges. So hauntingly majestic they were. So sacred was the feel of the silent surround. Something was happening. A Presence was approaching.

Eventually we continued our journey and pulled in at Bogan Flats Campground, which was deserted this time of year. We three were the only humans there among the drifting mist that rose and fell among the high evergreens. The only sound, the surging waters of the rushing Crystal River.

Because we were still psychically enthralled with the holy atmosphere of the place, we each walked off to experience solitude among the pines. Why I kept my eye on our friend, I don't know, but I felt the need to watch over her. I saw her snap her head around, as one does when another calls out to them. I looked around the deserted campground. No one else was there. Then I saw her knees begin to buckle and I raced to her, calling for Bill at the same time.

When we reached her she was going down. We held her up and supported her to a picnic bench. After she regained some measure of strength, she looked about. Bringing her eyes back to meet ours, she whispered, "Did you hear it?"

Bill and I exchanged glances.

"Hear what?" I asked.

"You didn't hear?" she puzzled.

We shook our heads.

"Someone spoke to me. The words were loud and clear."

"What was said?" I inquired.

Vickie's expression was nearly angelic. "YOU MUST COME HERE." She was shaking. "What does it mean? Who said that?

Can you find out who said that? Right afterwards. . .right after the words. . .I felt this incredibly warm love wrap around me. Oh, it was so beautiful!"

I checked for an answer.

"Gabriel. The voice came from the Archangel Gabriel. And. . .and the love that overwhelmed you was the touch of God."

Bill and I hugged our friend. She'd been moved to tears by the touch and was still crying.

I wondered at the event. So few people actually felt God's own touch. Few were so directly communicated with. Few were given such touchable verification of their direction. This was truly a major move by The White Brotherhood. Not that They caused the event, but that the event itself served to underscore our friend's direction which They were attempting to prompt her toward. What had happened was the epitome of spiritual communication and guidance. Never could our friend receive such a High message without it being verification of her destined path. Both Bill and I were ecstatic that her way had been made so clear.

"Oh-h-h yes," she sighed, "this is where I belong!"

After a time, we continued our journey along the road to Marble and stopped to show her the property. She too was in awe of the feeling of Starborn presences she'd felt there. Not just the property alone, but the entire area.

During the long drive back to Woodland Park, we were, for the most part, silent. Each was lost in the experience along the Crystal River. When conversation did pass between us, it was Vickie who spoke of a man she'd met while visiting the Southwest. She'd been drawn to him and expressed some contradicting thoughts that confused us. Vickie, contemplating a divorce, planned on her and her daughter relocating to Colorado, so why this talk of the Southwest? We let it go.

The following evening, Bill visited Vickie for a reason I knew nothing about. He'd been having strong impressions that I was to die soon. These impressions were, unbeknownst to me, verified by me when he asked me for an answer from our Advisors to a question he never voiced aloud. He just wanted a Yes or No answer. It was a Yes. So he received verification that proved his death impression about me was correct and it deeply disturbed him. He'd been pondering the probability in his mind. How would he go on without me? What would he do? How could he live alone? Would he even want to? Yet completing his work here was important. He knew he couldn't leave this world without doing his best. So how could he do what he had to do without someone beside him? His only answer was to have another to lean on. A friend who cared. Someone with a past-life connection who might be able to reconnect with true compassion and support until he regained his feet. Was this one of the reasons Vickie was being directed to Colorado? Was she the one chosen to be his shoulder to lean on when I left? Would she be the one to hold him up for a time? And he went to ask her.

She rejected him. She would not be his shoulder.

Bill returned home, saying that he'd helped her with one of her problems. He never whispered a word of his own heartache caused by her rejection.

A week later, after Vickie had returned home, he was again on the phone counselling her. As I passed through the office, I was engulfed in a heaviness that weighed my spirit. Though I was deeply concerned, I didn't interrupt their conversation.

When he got off the phone, he staggered into the living room. Tears were streaming down his face.

I guided him over to the couch and turned down the lights. I held him while he sobbed.

"After all she's been shown, how can she take the easy physical path? After Gabriel and God Himself made His presence known to her, how can she just brush that off? Oh God, I feel so sick inside. How can people be shown the way so clearly and still ignore and reject God's own signs?"

I held his hand. "What did she say?"

"She's complaining about the cold winters here. She doesn't like shoveling snow. She wants to go to the Southwest instead."

Now it was clear. Our friend opted for her gentleman friend instead of where she was being guided to be. Now I felt the depth of Bill's pain and attempted to comfort it.

"All you can do is give suggestions and share whatever our Advisors see for anyone. You've brought her into our circle with open arms. You've given her valuable insights and shown her where her future lies. And you say you've failed? Honey. . .she's failed herself! Don't you see that? A physician does all she can for her patients, but still some die. A psychiatrist talks and talks to clients, and still some go home and commit suicide. What more could you have done? Even Gabriel manifested his voice to her over there. God Himself made His presence known to her there and still she ended up rejecting all she'd heard and felt. Honey, if *God* and Gabriel couldn't get through to her, how is it you feel *you've* failed?"

He gave me such a devastatingly defeated look, then sobbed, "I don't know. I just felt she was such a close friend. She was *supposed* to be part of our future purpose and she threw it all away for an easier, more attractive physical path. I just tried for so long and it hurts so much to see a close friend turn away from God's own sign. I can't believe she began rationalizing about the weather. Her logic was so superficial!"

"You know that's what people do," I said.

"Oh, God!" he moaned through running tears.

I was out of words to comfort him with so great was his deep grief over this.

Then I felt the presence of Bill's Advisor coming closer and closer. I psychically moved over a bit and made room for him to share my consciousness.

The wisdom that issued forth was profound in its gentle comfort. The logic was high and impeccable.

Bill was told that he'd given too much of himself this time and that was why he hurt so badly now. He was told that his Heart Gate was wide open. He was also told to never counsel another person on a one-on-one basis like that again, for that aspect of his purpose was now over. He was told that a new purpose was waiting for him after he experienced a transition time.

By the time Bill's Advisor finished talking to him, more than an hour had passed. And, although Bill still remained in an extremely emotionally fragile state, I could see he felt much better.

As I sat beside him I could sense a "healing" being given to him. I can't describe what I felt, but it was perceived as a "cushioning" type of activity that was being generated from within him and radiating outward.

"Can you feel anything going on inside?" I whispered to him.

"My heart feels funny."

"Like how?"

"I can't describe it. It just feels funny."

"Bill, they're beginning to pass Time over your heart. They've already begun the healing."

Tears came to his eyes again. "They told me they were going to send a final message to Vickie tomorrow morning. They want us to completely disconnect with her because there's nothing more we can do to help her."

I didn't stay up to write in my Journal that night, instead I went to bed with Bill and held him until he finally fell to sleep. He'd worked so hard with our friend and given so, so much of himself. I knew he'd also felt rejected and betrayed. These feelings, piled on top of the "failure" he felt, were a powerful weight nobody's heart should have to endure.

The following morning I sat at the typewriter and closed my eyes. Soon a letter was before me and Bill mailed it Federal Express. The Brotherhood had had their final say.

The family was sympathetic with the situation. Jenny brought flowers home from the grocery store for her dad. She didn't quite understand all that had transpired the night before; all she knew was that Dad was hurting real bad inside and wanted to do something to make it better. Sarah and Aimee had showered him with warm, meaningful hugs throughout the day.

When Vickie received the Brotherhood's missive, a friend of hers called us to rage at Bill.

Bill, although he hurt, tried to gently explain. "These are very critical times and those in the Brotherhood do not fool around. They're *very* strict. They have no patience for people who play mind games, snow themselves, or rationalize their actions through defense mechanisms." Bill then explained about the incident involving our friend. "Because she flatly rejected signs from Gabriel and God, and chose a more attractive and easier path—her ultimate decision negated any further connection with us for the future and the Advisors saw how futile all my months and months of counseling had been."

Vickie's friend hung up on Bill.

In the early evening of December 31, 1991, while Bill was busy with a long consultation call, we received seven packages at our door. The seventh package was from Hampton Roads. It contained returned envelopes from their mailing. These were sent back to us so we could update people's addresses. As I glanced through the pile I came across one from Vickie. Her returned envelope was hastily written on. She never wanted to receive anything from Hampton Roads ever again!

I showed the envelope to Bill. The girls were in the office at the time and they felt sorry for Vickie when they saw what she'd written.

"She still blames you guys, doesn't she," Aimee concluded.

"Guess so," Bill sighed.

And I put the envelope back in the pile. The next day our friend's name would be permanently deleted from our mailing list—as requested.

Later Aimee came up to me. Vickie's returned envelope had been on her mind. "I can't believe that after all you and dad did for her she still blames you. She was the one who wanted to change her path. She was the one who wanted to go ahead and do what she wanted. I don't get why you're the bad guys here. It makes no sense for her to hate. . ."

"Forget it, Aimee," I smiled.

"But you guys even sent her money so she could have a Thanksgiving dinner and dad spent hours on the phone helping her with. . ."

"Doesn't matter now."

"What do you mean it doesn't matter now?"

I held up our friend's envelope.

"Well it's not fair," she spouted.

"Who's talking about fair? I'm talking *finished,* as in The End. If we're still the Bad Guys and she never wants to hear about any of my books, then we have to respect that. Okay?"

No response came.

"Okay, Aimee?"

Before she turned away, she grumbled, "It's still not fair. It's just not right."

Our girls were getting some invaluable lessons in relationships and the importance of not opening your heart, home, and
soul to someone who may later rip them to shreds.

Before Aimee went to bed that night, she came up to me
again.

"I just want to know one thing."

"Shoot."

"It's about Vickie. You don't still offer up your Prayer
Smoke for her, do you?"

"Yes."

She sighed. "Somehow I knew you'd say that. Why?"

"Why? Because I wasn't the one who wrote that letter, that's
why. That was our Advisors' doing."

"Give me another reason—the *real* one."

I raised a brow. "Is there another?"

"Yes."

"Aimee, when you spend such a long time helping someone
out, they become very close to you. You can't just cut that
person out of your heart. I still pray for her because I still
care."

Aimee was taken aback by that. "Even after what she wrote
on her returned envelope?"

"Even then. Think about it. You tell me what my spiritual
attitude should be."

She didn't have to think on it.

"Oh God, mom, I hate it when you're so logical."

"Goodnight, Aimee."

"Goodnight, mom."

And that night, because it was fitting to do so, my Prayer
Smoke rose for two people who turned cold hearts toward us.
For Vickie and her friend. Their names were whispered into
the rising smoke. . .because *I* still cared.

[End of deleted journal entry]

The above incidents with our close friend Vickie were deleted
when her friend called Bob at Hampton Roads to say we'd be
sued if we included the events in my Journal. However, the
depth of spiritual and heart pain that they caused Bill never
waned as was expected over time. The seed wedged within his

heart and festered as it grew into a grotesque, misshapened shadow that darkened our days for years to come. It planted in him a deep desire to find the one person who, he believed, had to come from outside our family group and have a pure and good heart. Someone who possessed unconditional love and could participate freely in such an emotional exchange of the heart. Someone, one person, out there who was elevated enough to be compassionate and loving enough to give to another without deferring to self. The seed and its resulting quest sent him into a one-minded tailspin that would twist and turn our lives inside out. . .it would become an all-consuming quest. . .a quest that sent him on a rollercoaster that soared him up to the highest heights, then plunged him down into the darkest depths of despondency. . .all for the purpose of his quest. . .looking for Goodheart.

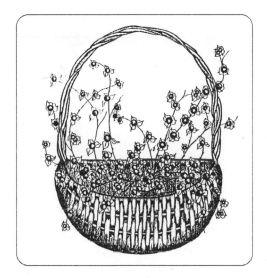

# THE CHANGELING HOUSE

*Note: Because our residence at this house lasted eighteen months and spawned emotional conflicts that lasted well into 1995, it was necessary to cover most of this time frame within this one story.*

1992 hadn't been half over and the year had already proven to be one packed with intense activities. The deposition and the three-day Metaphysical Fair were behind us. We hoped we'd have a few months of quiet respite before anything else demanded our time and energies.

Dreamers we were.

One problem that developed was with Bill. The entire family had commented on how irritable he seemed. He'd nitpick over the littlest things. He'd nag and badger us about being aware and attending to details. Our shared office space began to feel strained from his now-frequent comments to me about not telling him what to do. Me tell him what to do? Well, I'd always given my opinion on our business dealings because, as my business partner, he had to be apprised of what I wanted to do about various aspects. Suddenly he turned that around. Now I was "always telling him what to do." I wasn't sure where that'd come from or how it began in the first place. All I knew was that we weren't getting along nearly as well as before. It bothered me. It bothered me a lot.

"What's wrong, Bill?" I tried to find out.

"Nothing!" came the sharp reply.

"Well, why do you keep saying that I'm telling you what to do?"

"Because you are!"

"Honey, what's bothering you?"

"Nothing. Nothing!" That became the standard response.

His nagging continued with everyone around him. He was short and critical most of the time. No one had an answer.

Around the beginning of May, our landlords sent notice that they were planning on returning from Germany and were going to move back into their house. Grand Central Station would no longer be our domicile, nor would it remain the popular stop-over for our Starborn family members anymore.

It appeared that the time had come to seriously think about that land we'd been dreaming about for so long. The family (all seven of us) had a meeting. We discussed what we could afford if we all pitched in a portion of the separate incomes. Aimee was working as a Certified Nurse's Assistant at a Colorado Springs hospital, Robin was still at the City Market deli and Bill and I had just turned over the children's book to Hampton Roads, so we went over and over budgets together. Nobody wanted to split up, which was a blessing, because there was no way Bill and I could afford to buy a house on our own. It would take our three individual incomes to make the payments on a place large enough for the seven of us to have some decent space for individual privacy.

Bill called our real estate friend, Jane Stiffler. He listed the criteria we desired for our prospective place and she got right on it. Within a few days she had four properties for us to view.

The night before we were scheduled to accompany Jane to see the places, Bill and I snuggled in bed and talked about how great it was to finally be out looking at homes. In the silvery moonlight that speared through our bedroom windows, we were like small children awaiting Santa's arrival. Bill wondered if we could someday get a horse. I envisioned cougar and owl walking with me in heavy woods. We talked about how wonderful it'll be to finally stop renting so we can fix up and have fun redecorating like we used to do together. We recalled how we'd painted, panelled, and wallpapered our former Michigan houses. We smiled at the prospect of sharing those activities once again.

We were up early the following morning. Excitement filled our hearts. We met Jane at her office and rode in her car to the first of the four houses she had lined up.

The first house was rejected out of hand because of its location. It wasn't an appropriate setting for me to journey out at night and meet with my special friends. The second house she took us to was it. We never bothered to see the last two she had keys for.

This perfect house was located off of Wildhorn Road, just a mile north of Florissant. It had a gate that opened onto a long, curving drive that went over a small stream, then snaked up around a high hill. At the top, the drive gently sloped down to a five-car garage. Why anyone needed that was beyond us and we all joked about it. This was not some ritzy suburb. This was not Beverly Hills. However, one bay was actually a workshop. The original builder/owner must've been into car repair or something along those lines. So that left a garage for Robin's Tracker, Aimee's pickup (which was our old one), and our van. The last bay was used for storage and such. So far so good. We each could shelter our vehicles—even though we thought the number of bays was silly to see in the mountains.

The house itself was laid out beautifully in respect to our criteria. Everyone had a separate space that was more than satisfactory. Robin and Mandy had the entire lower floor which offered them a living room with moss rock fireplace, two sets of sliding patio doors that offered a beautiful mountain view, a wet bar to use as their private kitchen area, a full bath, separate entrances, and a large bedroom that they shared. Jenny and Aimee each had a bedroom on the main floor, and Sarah had her own across from ours on the top floor. Space was perfect!

As I describe this house now, it must sound enormous. It wasn't. It was just laid out right for us. On the second floor (or main level) there was a little sitting room with another double set of glass doors leading onto a large deck. This, I envisioned, would be my native room/office. I'd work there during the day and, by night, perform my Vision Way Ceremony and Prayer Smoke times. This was perfect for my quiet meditations and the solitude I required.

Bill and I were jumping out of our skins to show the place to the rest of our family. We chose a day when everyone was available and took them out to see it. They were all thrilled, especially with the privacy of its location—nearly forty acres of heavy pine and aspen woods covered the property on three sides. The only other house within miles was a place across the ravine and that too was for sale. Since one of our friends had expressed a great desire to purchase a mountain place (for the coming Changes), he ended up being our neighbor. So we didn't have to be concerned about hunters or dog breeders moving in next to us.

With a Giveaway from our friend to help with our down payment, we made a good offer for the place. The owner also owned several other large parcels of property in the Florissant area, including the Fossil Inn. We dickered over a few contractual points and, with those settled, quickly came to an agreement. We would do the owner-carry loan with no problem. We closed the deal on May 22nd and began moving in the same day.

Home! We were finally HOME!

While we were settling in, Bill made one request of me. He wanted me to hold off involving him in any redecorating work. He said he needed rest time before getting involved in any major projects. That was fine with me. Whatever I wanted to do, I could manage doing myself. And I did. I repainted five rooms and wallpapered them. I put up Z-Brick in the dining room and kitchen, and refinished some of the knotty pine panelling in my native room. . .all accomplished without asking Bill to lift a finger.

He ended up having quite a few small projects of his own to attend to. Man things; like making sure the fireplaces were cleaned and safe to operate, arranging all his tools in the garage workshop (they'd been in boxes since 1977 when we moved here), keeping the water well and septic system in top condition, doing some water witching to connect underground water lines (he's great at witching!). Anyway, little projects kept popping up for him to handle and there was no way he had any time to have "fun" painting and wallpapering. Although he was always busy with something, he never seemed to be as happy with "being settled" as he could've been. "It's nice," he'd comment. Naturally, being so close to him, this attitude lessened my own joy. What was the matter? I wondered. Why wasn't he filled with joy over being settled? Isn't that what we'd talked and dreamed about since 1977? Was *getting* one's dream— reaching the goal—a light that paled compared to the antici- pation of it? I couldn't believe that, not after waiting for so long. No, I couldn't believe that.

I frequently approached him. "What's wrong, honey?"

"Nothing."

Right.

"Please tell me what's wrong. You're not real happy here."

He'd keep repeating his standard reply until I got under his skin. Then he'd finally say, "You wouldn't understand."

"I wouldn't understand what? How do you know I wouldn't understand if you don't try to explain it to me."

He'd get irritated with the discussion. "Drop it. I said you wouldn't understand."

And I'd drop it. I'd drop it and watch him continue his days being critical of us and constantly nagging about being aware and the necessity of each of us attending to the details of our own lives. He complained about having to do everything for everyone—having to *think* of everything and handle everyone's details.

Well. . .he really didn't have to do those things. It was just always his mind for details that drove him to give attention to everyone else and make sure they were handling things them- selves. He could've saved himself a lot of stress if he *didn't* mind so many details.

On June 16th, I opened a correspondent's letter and was floored with her offer of a horse. I read the letter to the family. Aimee thought the idea was nice. Jenny didn't really care one way or the other. However, Sarah was ecstatic, I was excited and Bill wondered if this was "his" horse he'd always envisioned riding in the forest. We accepted. Bill contacted the owner and arrangements were made for transportation. The Morgan gelding, Valor, wouldn't arrive until the morning of August 18th. Preparations began.

The last garage bay had to be converted into a stall. A fenced corral had to be put up. Supplies bought. And a ton of learning to pack in—we didn't know the first thing about horses or how to care for them. None of us had had any kind of training as far as riding went. We were complete novices. We were ignorant from the word Go, but we did love horses, and that love turned into a determination to have the best cared-for horse west of the Mississippi.

Bill went on an information-gathering quest. He spoke to seasoned ranchers and long-time friends who were horse people. One of Sarah's school friends rode in the annual rodeo and had amassed trophy upon trophies. We bought books. We talked to the owners of ranch supply shops. We were sure our Valor was going to come home to loving and caring people.

Bill worked hard. He drafted Sarah as his helper. They renovated the last garage bay into a fine stall. When Valor did arrive and our vet came out to check him over, he said that our stall set-up was like a horse being at the Ritz! That made us feel good about all the work we'd done. Dr. Joel Stahlecker also looked over the corral. He shook his head. "This horse has got the best set-up in the county!" That made Bill proud. He and Sarah had worked day and night getting it up right.

And speaking of the corral fencing. . .this project took several weeks to accomplish and, all the time, Bill shouted and swore at Sarah while they worked. More times than I like to recall, she came running into the house, slamming the door. "I'm *not* helping him any more!" she'd complain with tears running down her cheeks. "What's *wrong* with him?"

I'd pull her to me and hug tight. "I don't know. He says I

wouldn't understand. I don't know why he's so irritable and crabby. It's not fair that he's always criticizing us for so much, but try to let it roll off your back. Your dad still loves you a lot. It's not you. I don't know what it is. Just try to help him as much as you can and ignore his swearing."

"But he's being so *mean* out there. I've never put up a wire fence before and neither has he. I don't know how much tension to keep and he keeps swearing at me. Why should I take that?"

I smoothed down her hair. "Sarah, you take it by overlooking it. You take it because you know he loves you. Something's bothering him. Something's changed him. We have to ride this out."

Sarah understood. She didn't like it, but she understood. And back outside she'd go. In the end, she learned to talk back and swear just as much as he did. He'd laugh at that and say, "I think I finally taught Sarah to come out of her shell and be assertive." And they'd joke about it. Underneath it all, everyone knew it was no joke. Something was wrong. Something was very wrong. Ever since moving into our new house, Bill was different; something was changing his whole personality.

Father's Day rolled around. Everyone had gifts for Bill, even Robin and Mandy. This was not the celebration of gaiety we normally experienced. This one was a little strained because of his change in attitude. Yet we smiled and laughed and presented our gifts. He smiled and laughed a little less believably.

The gift that seemed most amusing turned out to be the singular one that changed him the most—for the worse. Aimee had presented him with something he'd never had. . .a gift certificate for a massage. For a while it sat on his desk. He'd call to make an appointment when he had time. It seemed so innocuous at the time. A unique gift that all of us were surprised over. Aimee had come up with something really different this time.

In July we had need of a repairman for the upstairs bathroom jacuzzi. We never used it because it took too much well water and we felt it too precious to waste on such a frivolous thing. However, after Bill had a particular exhaustive work day, he wanted to relax his sore muscles, so we tried to work it. Once started, it wouldn't turn off. We decided the thing just wasn't worth it yet still wanted it to be in working order. The wiring seemed to be wrong and we feared a short or fire.

The repairman who came out was young. He looked like he'd just come from Surf City in Malibu. I didn't like the impressions I got when I let him in the door.

Bill was in town when this young man came. I hate to say it, but I despise handling these situations alone. I'm shy to begin with and don't like having to talk to strangers who come over. I showed the young man the jacuzzi and left him to do his thing.

The following morning, when I went into the bathroom to put on my new wedding ring. . .it was gone from the shelf. There were my other two rings that were turquoise, but no little diamond in the flower setting. I couldn't believe it. After waiting so many years to replace my wedding rings and after just getting them, they disappear from the shelf. Disappear? Nothing else was missing. Why just the diamond?

I rushed downstairs. "Bill! That guy stole my wedding rings!"

Bill, ever the trusting soul, responded, "That's kinda strong. You sure they didn't slip back behind the shelf? You sure you left them with the others?"

I explained how I'd taken them all off when I put suntan oil on. I'd placed them in one place. They were all there except for the wedding rings. "That guy was up there alone. He *took* them! Call the shop and tell them." Bill always handled telephone calls for me because I hated using the phone. This time he was not about to make some wild accusation.

"Let's wait a few days. Meanwhile, you look around good. Maybe you forgot and left them somewhere else."

I was furious. "He *took* them! I *know* he did. If we wait he's gonna sell them! I'll never see them again!"

"I'm not calling, Mary. Just wait a few days."

I was fuming. I waited. I searched. Nothing.

Finally Bill called the shop. The owners were disturbed by the incident and said they'd speak with the repairman. A call-back assured us that their man did not steal any rings.

"Liar!" I said. "That kid's lying! He *took* it, I *know* he did!"

"Okay," Bill said, "I'll call him at home and confront him personally."

"How are you going to do that?"

"I've got his name. We'll see if he has a home phone," he said, pulling the phone book from his desk drawer. And he found it.

I listened to the one-sided conversation. I was not pleased with what I heard.

When Bill hung up the receiver, I was ranting before he could open his mouth. "He's lying through his teeth."

"Honey. . ." he tried.

"Don't 'honey' me! He TOOK it! He's a *thief!* "

I began to cry.

"After waiting so many years to replace those rings this is what happens to them. I can't believe it. I just can't believe they're gone. I'll never get them back. They meant so much to me."

He held me. "We'll replace them."

Although his intentions were good, we had no money then to do any replacing of anything.

When the telephone rang and he became involved with a business call, I walked out of the room. I walked through the house and looked around at it. What was it? What was I feeling from these walls? I whispered to them.

"You're doing something, aren't you. You're doing something and you know exactly what you're doing." It was then when the strong impression came over me that this was not our dream house at all. This was a Place of Transition for us. . .a Way Station. . .a place where changes had to take place in order for us to continue our mission with clarity. This was the Stop-over Station where we had to leave all our excess baggage behind. And I wondered, was Bill's changed personality a part of this transition? Was he working on leaving some damaged baggage behind? And was he having trouble setting it down and walking away from it?

It hurt to think that our long wait to be settled turned out to be only a House of Transition. . .a Changeling House where certain aspects of our lives and personalities needed clearing. It hurt to think that perhaps we'd never be settled. Perhaps we never were meant to be. One thought led to others. Messengers don't return to be settled, they come to do work. When the work is finished, they leave. What's to be settled? Where the messenger lives is not germane. No, not relevant at all. I then realized that the word "settled" had no meaning for us. We'd be settled wherever we were at any one time. My last thought that day was one that came with a wry smile. How tricky Destiny was. . .how very tricky to cleverly lead us to a Place of Transition that we foolishly thought was our dream come true. We never stop learning, do we.

When the same repairman came again to the house, he brought a new motor to install. Again I was alone with him. This time I followed him up to our bathroom and glared at him the entire time he was working. I had the distinct feeling that he was so unaware that my intensity didn't faze him one bit. At least it made me feel good to be doing *something*. Bill eventually reported it to the sheriff.

A few months later, the shop called us. They wanted more detailed particulars regarding our accusation of their man. It seemed that he'd ripped them off and stolen some equipment. They had an actual robbery with broken windows and all. And the young surfer had flown the coop.

I didn't say a word to Bill. I never said, "I told you so." I didn't have to.

Bill cashed in his massage gift. When he returned, he talked to me about how sensitive the massage therapist was. *Cassie worked in Woodland Park and was familiar with my books. She was involved in a spiritual group that met every so often.

Bill, being the intense extrovert that he is, gets a real high meeting with aware and metaphysically-involved folks. He praised Cassie for her awareness and asked me if I'd autograph some books for her. That was never a problem. I was always happy to gift people with signed books.

Soon Bill began seeing Cassie for the purpose of counselling her regarding her relationship with her husband. They were having a few problems and Bill was eager to assist. He was exceptionally perceptive when it came to people's psychological aspects and was darn good at getting to the root of their subconscious troubles. Eventually Cassie invited him to her home so he could talk to her and her husband together. The three of them got along well. Bill thought her husband was a good man, and the three of them talked about the four of us going out to dinner some time. Although we never managed time for this, Bill spent a lot of time helping her with various issues of concern. This new activity gave him a renewed spiritual high. He loved helping people. However, he still had something nagging at him. He remained critical of those at home. He still struck out at those who loved him most. And, unbeknownst to any of us, he was still hurting inside from Vickie and beginning to slip into a major mid-life crisis.

I'd not done any redecorating in several months. The one project I had left was to half-panel the dining room and hallway. I liked the look of wainscotting and we'd chosen a paneling that had the look of deer, rabbits, and cabins woodburned into it. The time had come to do the deed. . .but we'd do the deed by ourselves and not involve dad.

So Jenny, Sarah, and I got the cut paneling out and all the supplies. We were going to do this little project while Bill was out working in the shop.

Just as I was about to wield the saw, in he came. "You can't do that kind of thing yourself," he said. "Here, let me help you with that."

"That's okay," Sarah immediately replied, "we don't want to take you away from whatever you're doing. We can handle this one."

He smirked. "Right. Hand me the saw."

And he picked up the saw. He began cutting. He grumbled when it didn't go right. He swore. He shouted at me, "Why do you have to *always* have to make work? Can't you live *anywhere* without *working* on the place? I told you I needed a rest!" He swore at me so much that tears began to silently roll down my face. When I tried to hide them, Sarah raged back at him

"Daddy! What the hell's the *matter* with you! You and mom always *talked* about fixing up your dream house! Why are you cussing at her? What's *wrong* with you?"

He swung around and glared at her. "Go to hell! I'm tired of fixing this place up!"

I shouted at him through the tears. "I never asked you to do one single thing. *I* painted five rooms. *I* worked to put the Z-Brick in the kitchen and dining room. *I* wallpapered three rooms and the hallway. *We* didn't *ask* you to help with this paneling. . .you *offered!*"

"The hell with this place!" he said, picking up a second sheet of paneling.

I ran into the bathroom and locked the door. I cried my eyes out. I mumbled between sobs. I just could not believe he was acting like he was and saying the things he was about our house. After waiting so many years to get settled it was turning out to be one nightmare after the other.

Sarah banged on the door and demanded to be let in. She wanted to comfort me.

I told her I needed to be left alone.

Out in the dining room, I heard him swearing and complaining more. The girls were being silent. They were letting him vent whatever it was that needed releasing. They were not pleased with how their dad was acting. They were not pleased with how he'd been acting ever since we moved in.

After I calmed somewhat, I returned to the dining room to do whatever I could to assist with the last project I'd ever do on the house I came to view as the Changeling House I hated.

A week or so later, Bill came home from an appointment with Cassie. "She helped me," he announced. He was genuinely happy that someone had helped him with his internal problem.

"How'd she help you?" I responded.

"She helped heal my heart pain."

"Your heart pain? Pain from what?"

"It's too complicated and you wouldn't understand. Just be happy for me. I feel so much better now."

Well, I was glad to hear that, yet felt I was being left out of something that was important in his life. What was it he thought I wouldn't understand? I kept asking, but he kept giving me the same response. "It's okay, you wouldn't understand anyway." So I let it ride. What was the use going around and around with it?

He asked me if he could bring Cassie to the house. She was having more marriage problems and wanted to know if I would help. He felt Cassie was uncomfortable with just him counselling her. He felt she had the impression I might resent his time with her. That was just plain silly. I never resented any time he spent with anyone he counselled. And he did a lot of it.

I naturally was glad to invite Cassie over to the house. We sat in my native room and talked for a while. She was interested in many of the native gifts correspondents had sent me and I showed them to her. I noticed that she was particularly drawn to a large statue of the winged Isis I had on top of one of the bookshelves. It was just something that I observed. She didn't verbalize much about it. We were soon off on other topics.

The next time Bill was scheduled to counsel Cassie, I told him to take the statue to her as a gift of appreciation from me for helping with his heart pain. Bill was flabbergasted. I assured him that it was okay. I wanted to do a little something for her. Actually, giving my things away gave me great pleasure and Bill knew that. He was excited to give it to her.

Later in the week, Bill was pleased to say, "Cassie has the statue in her massage room and one client said that it gave the room a wonderful warm feeling. . .a peaceful aura."

I was happy to hear that. I didn't realize she'd place it in her working area, but I guess that's where she was inclined to put it.

As time passed, Bill spent more and more time counselling Cassie and she, in turn, did energy work for his heart center. It was getting to be so often that the girls were becoming concerned. They didn't like him being gone all the time. They thought it wasn't right. Their dad seemed to rave a little too much about Cassie and how grateful he was for what she'd done for him. Relationships became strained between him and the girls. I tried to reassure them until I too felt a little left out of his life. Finally I suggested he cut down the frequency of their meetings. He took this as me "telling" him what to do. It didn't go over well. . .not well at all. He overreacted. He went to see her and told her he wouldn't be seeing her anymore. When he pulled up into the garage, I'd just finished stacking a cord of wood. I noticed that it took him a long time to come out of the garage. When he did, he was staggering. I ran up to him. He was not lucid. He was confused and unsteady. He couldn't support himself.

"What did you take," I asked, while supporting him up the steps.

"Some pills. It hurt to say goodbye. I didn't want to hurt."

Oh God, he'd taken an overdose of his prescription pills.

I helped him up the stairs and into the house. I got him in bed. "How much did you take?"

"I don't know."

I was silent for a moment while I checked for the information I needed. Our Advisors quickly responded.

Sarah came running into the bedroom. She was scared for her dad.

"He'll be all right," I whispered. "He'll be able to sleep it off, but he won't feel so good when he wakes up."

We made him comfortable, then left.

When he recovered, he was crabbier than ever. Nothing we did was right anymore. He nitpicked. He swore at us. He complained about everything. Eventually the family began to avoid him as much as possible. This was the only way we could exist without being barked at for something. He was slipping deeper into his mid-life crisis.

Me? I'd escape by going out into the woods at night. I had to get some measure of peace. I had no idea what was wrong. Confusion reigned with a heavy hand. Our household was being torn and ripped and I'd look through tears up between the sweet pine boughs and ask, "Why!"

This Changeling House also affected me. My cougar and owl didn't come near it. I was completely alone since moving in. My Starman stayed away too. No visitors of any kind came to comfort me. It was as if I was cast adrift to learn to swim for myself. No warm companionship from my old and dear friends. No guidance anymore. No sweet moments of loving were shared. I was so alone. I was so, so alone. Oh yes, by now I knew why I was all alone. It was because Bill and I needed to shed baggage before advancing to the next stage of our mission. It was to make us both stronger through personal adversity. These difficulties we didn't need. These we experienced just the same. And I began to hate this Changeling House that was so void of love and companionship. I began to hate the whole space I was thrust within. It was a complete void. A lifeless, airless space that seemed to have no rhyme or reason to it.

We existed. Together, the family worked and breathed and occupied one dwelling. More I cannot say about it.

Thanksgiving came. What was always a time of great joy and gatherings with friends, became a very strained affair. Everyone but Bill put much energy into seeming to be fine. We made a valiant effort. However, at dinner, Bill began to pick on Aimee for something. Then he directed berating comments to Sarah. I couldn't believe he'd spoil our Thanksgiving dinner. People left the table.

I was in tears. "Bill," I said, "you've got to tell me what's bothering you." I figured he still thought I wouldn't understand.

"*I* don't have to tell *you* anything. Why do you pick on me? Why don't *you* ever talk to the girls about doing what they're supposed to be doing? Why do *I* always have to keep the details and make sure things get done around here?"

"What are you talking about? They do okay at taking care of their own business. I just want to know why you're so crabby all the time. Did you *have* to spoil our Thanksgiving dinner?"

He sneered at me. "Oh sure, I'm the one to blame. I'm always the one you blame. It's always me, isn't it."

All I could do was look at him. I had no response to how easily he could twist things. I had no recourse but to turn and begin to clear away the dishes. The girls came back to help. No one spoke. There were more and more of those black days and nights when no one spoke. . .but only when *he* was around. When he wasn't, the girls and I had a wonderful relationship. . .except when I could see they felt sorry for me. I felt sorry for me too. I felt sorry for all of us. Mostly for Bill.

Bill became more and more depressed. More often than not, he'd escape the family by going to bed early—very early. One such evening, while I was alone in the house and in my native room making my preparations for the Prayer Smoke time, I had an awful sinking feeling. I felt compelled to go upstairs and check on Bill.

I got up and ran up the stairs. Half way up, all the smoke alarms in the house went off. A hard shiver raked through me. Throwing open the bedroom door, I saw him lying in bed with the small headboard light shining through the glass. I raced over to him.

Ignoring the blaring alarms, I bent down to him. "Are you al. . ." My scalp crawled.

He was holding a loaded gun.

"BILL! Give that to me!" And I grabbed for it.

"No!" he shouted back over the buzzing racket.

I managed to get my hands on the barrel and yanked it my way.

He held tight onto the handle, finger crooked around the trigger.

We fought over it.

Finally, his grip relaxed.

I lifted it away.

The smoke alarms stopped.

I sat beside him. I sighed. "Do you really want to leave me?" I quietly cried.

Silence.

"Honey?"

Silence.

I rested the gun against my chest in order to lie beside him. I nestled it where he couldn't readily grab for it. "Bill, I love you so much. Your girls love you deeply. We're the only people in the world who love and care for you. We'd be heartbroken if you weren't here with us. Do you know that?"

He groaned. "I know that," came the soft reply.

"I'd die without you, Bill." Tears were flowing from my eyes. "Do you know that too? I'd wither away and die without you. Please let me help you."

"You wouldn't understand," came the whispered reply.

Oh, how I cringed every time that response came. I just cringed. "I could try. I could try to understand. How can I help you if you won't tell me what's wrong?"

He sighed. "I won't leave you," he softly said as tears formed in the corners of his eyes. "I really couldn't do that to you."

A few quiet moments passed.

"What's making you so depressed? What's causing this terrible blackness you have around you?"

He turned his head to look at me. The look was one of someone lost. "It's not around me. The blackness. . .the blackness is *in* me. It's in my heart."

I hugged him with my free arm. "Please tell me. Please let me in."

He shook his head. He just shook his head and told me he'd be okay now. I felt like I'd been dismissed. I kissed his forehead and left the room with the gun.

Downstairs, I took our other guns and hid them all. He did say he'd never leave me. I was just making sure.

I returned to my room, lit the herbs, and began to pray my heart out as the smoke began to rise up the chimney and out into the dark night.

The Christmas season was upon us. Things hadn't gotten much better. Bill was still deeply depressed over something I couldn't help him with because he couldn't tell me because I wouldn't understand. What I couldn't understand was the logic of the whole thing. I desperately wanted to help him. My hands were tied. Though we all attempted to assist him, much of the time we just left him alone.

His attitude never wavered. Our efforts to help him weren't effective. We began to feel like we were nothing but major irritations to him.

Christmas Eve came. We all gathered in my native room where we had the tree lit. We smiled and laughed. We opened gifts. Bill excused himself. . .he said he had a bad headache. We could see he was not enjoying himself. He was not at all happy.

Christmas Day was not much better. The family went through the motions of celebrating. I fixed a nice dinner which turned into a disaster that scattered family members away from the room when Bill began to nitpick at them. I'd had it. I couldn't take anymore of this devastating discord. I confronted him.

"Did you have to spoil Christmas?"

"Is that all you care about? What about *me*?"

"I've been *asking* about you ever since we moved in! You refuse to tell me anything about you! It's time you talked about whatever's bugging you. You've been cruel to us. You either ignore us or else criticize us all the time. You treat us like we're nothing but *irritants* in your life. Bill! You act like you don't *love* us!"

His response was cold. "Do *you* love *me*?"

"What's that supposed to mean? You know we love you. Nothing's changed with *us*—it's *you* that's changed!"

"Yeah, I've changed. I've changed because I've been *hurting* for eighteen months and nobody wants to help me. I feel all alone."

I was incredulous. "Hurting! How can we *help* you if we don't know you're hurting!"

Silence.

"Bill? How did you expect us to help when no one knew?"

"I couldn't tell you."

I was getting lost. He'd left me in his mental dust. I sat at the half-cleared dining table trying to figure this out. He was mad at us for not helping the hurt he felt. Okay. But then he says he couldn't *tell* us he was hurting. So if we didn't know because he couldn't tell us, how can he blame us for not helping him? I had the scary feeling that maybe I was going crazy. I looked up at him. He was standing in the kitchen. Arms crossed. Leaning against the counter. So cool. Cold. So calm. Cold. So sure. Sane?

I sighed. Was his logic sound and mine confused? I certainly was confused. I was more confused than I'd ever been in my life. "Am I missing something here?" I asked.

"I don't know, are you?" he replied.

He sounded like a robot. No feeling. Just cold.

I scratched my head. "Bill, either I'm going crazy or you're not making any sense. Let me try and get this straight. You're saying that you blame us. . ."

"You. I blame *you*."

"Well, okay. You're blaming *me* for not helping you with your heart pain. Right?"

"Right."

"Okay. And I couldn't help you with it because I didn't know about it. Right?"

"You *should've* known about it."

"Alright. But I didn't know about it because you couldn't tell me." I looked to him for verification.

He nodded.

"So if I didn't *help* you because I didn't *know* about it because you couldn't tell me, I guess I need to know *why* you couldn't tell me."

"Because you wouldn't be understanding."

That's it. That. . .was. . .IT!

"And you've been BLAMING me all these months for something I couldn't HELP you with because you couldn't TELL me because I wouldn't BE understanding?"

He calmly nodded. He nodded calmly as if everything I'd just said made perfect sense.

Now I *knew* I was going crazy. I sat in utter silence for a long while.

He stood at the counter.

Suddenly my hair stood on end. "It's her, isn't it," I whispered in defeat. "It's been Vickie all along."

The response was cold. "I told you you wouldn't be understanding."

I looked up at his ice blue eyes. "It *is* her. *She's* the cause of all this." Tears began to come. "I can't believe you'd ever let anything or anyone come between us. You are the most important person in my life—nothing could take precedence over our love. I can't believe you hated me all these months because of not helping you with the pain she caused you. You never even let on she was still hurting your heart. You held onto that pain all these months. And you blamed me. You let her come between us and what we dreamed of for years and years. You let her turn our dream into a nightmare—a living hell for the whole family."

"I told you you wouldn't understand."

"Oh, I understand perfectly." And I went into the native room to sit in my reading chair. I was stunned. Absolutely stunned. I couldn't think of anything other than the ugly fact that he'd let something take priority over our love—something I never believed possible. Someone else causes him great heart pain and he blames me for it. Was I truly crazy that I couldn't understand this logic that seemed so clear to him? All I could think of was how he'd let something or someone come between us. How could he truly love me if he allowed that to happen?

Well? He must not really love me then. Yes, that was it, wasn't it? He no longer loved me enough to endure anything for that love. He no longer loved me. . .he no longer loved me. . .he no longer loved. . .I ran upstairs. I ran into the bathroom and stood before the mirror. "He no longer loves me," I whispered at the red-eyed reflection. Slowly my gaze lowered to the counter. In one swift swipe, I wiped it clean. Everything went flying. Glass broke against walls and the jacuzzi. "HE DOESN'T LOVE ME! HE DOESN'T LOVE ME! OH, *GOD!* HE DOESN'T *LOVE* ME ANYMORE!" I cried and cried as I looked for more to vent my rage out on.

Suddenly arms were around me. Robin and the girls had come to my aid. Robin escorted me into the bedroom. She thought I was headed toward the bed to lie down. But when I got beside the bedside table, I spied the Victorian lamp. In one flash, I'd cleaned off the table. Glass smashed across the room. The herb vase went along with it. I'd taken them by surprise.

I ran to the top of the landing.

Down below, Bill stood and looked up.

"HE DOESN'T LOVE ME!" I kept crying.

He spoke to the others. His voice was cold. "See? She's just thinking of herself. She doesn't care about me."

"What?" I whispered down to him. "What did you just say?"

He shook his head and went down into Robin's living area.

As in a slow-motion dreamstate, I slowly descended the stairs. I was numb. I walked into the native room and began taking the decorations off the tree. This was Christmas Day. Christmas was over. This year it was over early. And Robin and the girls brought the Christmas trimming boxes up from the storage room. Together, in silence, we dismantled the tree and cleared the room of all holiday evidence. This year, Christmas never came. At least not for me.

The new year came. I hoped new beginnings would also enter our lives. This didn't prove to be true, for Bill slumped further and further into his pain of the mid-life crisis in which he questioned his entire life, his purpose, his self-worth.

Bill remained distant and frequently deeply depressed. Relationships between family members were strained. On the whole, we tried to avoid Bill as much as possible so as to avert any sort of confrontation. There were some fair days—sweet ones. There were days when our smiles and laughter were genuine. And there were the bitter ones. On the whole, though, things were chilled and grey.

One evening, when Jenny and Aimee were gone and Robin and Mandy were also out, Bill slipped into a mood that was blacker than I'd ever seen him in. He ranted about everything under the sun. He was scaring me. I went to Sarah and told her to lock herself in her room. I feared for what her dad might do, so strange was his behavior. Although he'd never laid a hand on us, and probably never would, this new mood frightened me anyway.

I was downstairs trying to write. He blustered down and stood in the doorway. He shouted and swore and raged. I went up to him and looked into his face. My hair stood on end.

This was not Bill.

This was some raging stranger I didn't know. He didn't even look like Bill!

I stood my ground before this stranger. His eyes were cold. I had the thought that no soul was behind them. My next thought was, this is what a cold-blooded killer looks like. I shivered just before all the smoke alarms went off again. All three, one on each floor began to blare at once.

The stranger flinched. He turned and walked up the stairs.

I grabbed my gun and pulled an Indian blanket off the couch on the way outside. If this stranger came after me I at least wanted to be outside where I was free to run for my life. I huddled beneath the deck. Soon afterward, Sarah snuck around to where I was. She was shaking.

"I'm scared," she whispered, when she saw I had my gun "That's not daddy in there. What's going on? Who is that?"

I had no answers. "I don't understand it any more than you do. We'll be okay out here. He doesn't know where we are." And I double-checked my pockets for the extra quick-loads I brought for the revolver. The Magnum was loaded with Black Talons. I shuddered at the thought of using them.

Suddenly we froze.

"Mary? Sarah? You two out there?" he called from the doorway.

Did the stranger have a gun in his hand? What was his mental state? Did he have a plan? Was this what it finally came down to? He and I facing each other with our deadly loaded guns? Oh, *God*, don't let it be so!

I eased around the corner of the house. My sights immediately checked his hands.

Empty.

"Hey, you two," he said, voice full of concern, "what're you doing out there? It's too cold to be out without jackets."

Sarah and I exchanged glances at one another. She was frowning. "Dad's back."

"Let's go inside," I said. "I think it's all over." Whatever It was, we didn't know.

Back inside the smoke alarms were silent.

Bill was standing beside Robin's couch.

Sarah and I walked in the room and Bill noticed my gun. He didn't say anything.

I set the blanket down.

Sarah faced us. She looked to her dad, then to me. "What just happened?"

I looked to Bill for the answer that I couldn't give.

He raked his hands through his hair. "I'm not sure, Sarah. I remember raging about something. God, I don't even know what about. I recall feeling really odd. . .like ice cold. . .like I could kill and never have any feelings about doing it. It scared me. Then I remember hearing the smoke alarms. They sounded far away, but just close enough to jar something inside me. I walked up the stairs and then the alarms were quiet. That's when I realized I was alone in the house." He looked at us. "I don't know what happened. I just don't know. All I do know is that I could never physically harm anyone in my family."

After that terrifying incident, things began getting better. The three battery-operated smoke alarms were silent for the remainder of our stay at the Wildhorn house. These, we noticed, had been mysteriously set off by unknown forces whenever a situation in our house was reaching a critical or dangerous point.

Eventually he went back to counselling Cassie, but on a very limited basis. He had a basic spiritual need to help people and this activity also assisted him in keeping his own mission active.

In March, he went to another massage therapy office in Woodland Park run by two ladies. He needed the work for his neck and back which bothered him often. The three soon became good friends and they shared some information with him— someone in town was spreading ugly rumors about him and his family.

What? What now?

Now it was Cassie who had turned on him behind his back. She'd told someone (who told others) that Bill had stalked her. She told the other massage therapists that he needed to be watched. She told people that Mary Summer Rain had given her a statue that had a hex on it. She told people Bill had a dysfunctional family.

Now Bill came home really upset. He wanted to prove Cassie wrong. He wanted to straighten all the lies out.

I tried to calm him down. "Honey, people tell tales about *me* all the time. They're lies, yeah, but I can't go around tracing every dumb rumor about me and busting butt trying to put things right. You have to expect this sort of thing. For one reason or another, people love spreading dirt about people like us."

"But this is about me!"

I raised a brow. "Oh? And that makes a difference?"

He smiled. "Well, sort of, I mean, this is right here in our own home town, for heaven's sake. We know a heck of a lot of people. Something crazy like this needs to be put down as fast as possible."

I sighed. I really didn't see the need. People gossiped and fed rumors all the time. It seemed like it was the All-American pastime. Something juicy made talk all the more interesting, did it not? Yet I saw his logic in this.

"Seems to me, though," I commented, "if it were true that you stalked her, wouldn't it also be true that she'd have filed a police complaint against you?"

"People don't think that deep," he added. "Besides, what bothers me is the confidentiality these massage therapists are supposed to have regarding their clients. She yaks lies about me to another therapist who, in turn, spreads the lies to *her* clients. Where's the professional attitude and ethics?" He sighed.

"And another thing, Cassie told this therapist that she refuses to have any contact with me. She had the nerve to say she hangs up on me whenever I call her. How can she say that when *she* calls *me*? For God's *sake,* we're on speaking terms right this minute! I'm really irked that she's done this behind my back and, to my face, she's still sweet as pie."

"Well, yeah, I can see how you'd be upset with such a double attitude," I grinned, "kinda like having a forked tongue."

He paced the floor. "I have to find a way to prove she's making up lies about us. There's got to be a way to show she's lying."

I didn't see how.

Then his eyes lit up. "Got it!"

"What!" I grinned.

"Cassie and I are still on good speaking terms. What if I give her a call just to see how things are going for her and her husband?"

I frowned. "Okay. . .you call. . .then what?"

"Well, I didn't tell you the rest. We have *witnesses* to the conversation."

Oh, he was clever. "That'd be great. Of course you should say something that dates it. That way you can prove she's still talking to you when she's telling people she's hanging up on you."

He thought that over. "She called me after that Fourth of July thing they went to. We talked for quite a long time. I could refer to her call about that. It was just a week or so ago."

And that's just what he did. We'd arranged a few witnesses to be present and they heard Cassie voluntarily keep the conversation with Bill going by asking about the girls and this and that. I got on the phone too. I asked her if she and her husband still wanted the four of us to go out to dinner some time. Oh yeah! was her reply.

When Bill hung up the phone, I heard an energetic, "Yes!"

The following day we took the news to our massage therapist friend who, in turn, relayed the witnessed phone conversation to the main gossip-monger. Our friends were anxious to ask her one thing.

Would she like to know the truth about Bill? Proof that was witnessed by several people? It turned out that this was not necessary. The fact that proof existed was enough to end it all.

What Bill figured out was that Cassie needed a way to cast aspersions against someone who had gotten too close to her psychological defenses. Bill had counselled her so much that he'd broken through her self-generated mind games and found the root problem. He had a knack for getting through people's facades. Some folks just couldn't deal with that. They created ways to get out of it. . .even if they were lies.

Bill was lucky in that he was able to dispel the ugly rumors about us. On the other hand, I'm not so fortunate. Consequently, I pray for those who spread false gossip about me. I've no other recourse, yet it may, ultimately, be the best recourse there is.

The Changeling House.

The Place of Transition.

The Way Station where we clear ourselves and leave the ragged baggage behind. This serious time frame for Bill obviously took place over many months, all the while, books were being written, death threats were coming in the mail, our horse came, our dog died—the rest of the Bittersweet book stories were being lived all intertwined with what transpired at the Changeling House.

As to the why of it, I can explain it better now through the wisdom and clarity of hindsight. Bill, being the highly emotional personality that he is, always exhibits a high sensitivity to individuals he's had past-life experiences with. As a completed spirit, his heart center—like mine—is thrown open at all times. This aspect makes people like us extra-sensitive to giving and receiving feelings of pure and unconditional love. Yet this is not all wonderful. It also opens the heart center to the deep and intense pain of rejection (spiritually and emotionally). This type of searing pain cannot be talked away, nor can it be medicated away. Bill's months of trying to deal with the pain caused him to be irritable with everyone around him. He lashed out at anyone within striking distance, like an injured animal who often strikes out and bites his owner who tries to help it. His pain was a consuming fire that roared so hot nobody close to him could get near him to help. Everyone was held away at arm's length while he searched for the one person outside the family who would give him the unconditional caring and compassion that would fill his heart with the warmth of pure love. That, he adamantly believed, was the only cure. That cure could only come from the one person he so desperately sought. . .Goodheart.

Although Bill had Goodheart standing beside him all the time, he never saw or felt her there. He looked far and wide for his idea of who Goodheart should be. Deep inside, he believed that his healing could only come from this outside person instead of the one who'd been standing beside him for twenty-nine years. In the end, neither of us understood why I wasn't seen at his side. I stood alone looking up at him while he stood alone looking out in the distance for Goodheart to approach. Both feeling very much alone and unloved.

It was an ugly time. A time of desperation. A time that forcefully pushed the limits of our relationship. A test of sanity and perseverance. Many other changes took place while living in the Wildhorn house; these are revealed in the following stories. Yet, because it was so emotionally important for Bill to locate that one special individual who he believed possessed true unconditional love and compassion, his search went on. At times this search drove him into a deep despondency over the fact that there seemed to be no one to fit the bill; other times he sorrowed over the appearance of the world containing no such human and he felt he was in search of an extinct mortal species. This thought depressed him to the point of wanting to end his life several times. It drove him to the brink of blinding rages at me. It drove him into what he called his "ice man" state where he felt completely emotionless. . .cold.

And the search for Goodheart continued. Why? It continued because his heart pain never totally went away. He still hurt from feeling he'd spiritually failed with Vickie. He still hurt from experiencing a past-life connection who rejected God's touch and Gabriel's voice. He still hurt because he'd cried his heart out to someone asking for a compassionate friend to lean on if I died and she turned to ice in his face. Although I had great compassion for his pain, I was also filled with mixed feelings for his attempt to secure emotional support before I was even dead. It didn't set well with me, yet I focused my attention on her rejection of his request. Initially I gave him comfort, but when the pain took hold for so long and ended up coming between us, I felt very much alone.

Eventually Bill's behavior became so depressive that I insisted he see a doctor. He was diagnosed with Male Midlife Crisis and given medication to ease his darker days. This helped for a while, but he still remained centered on his search for Goodheart. It was a search that would drive an iron wedge between us. It was a search that would nearly destroy me while I stood watching and waiting for it to end. It was a search that kept my own stabbing heart pains silent while I accepted a situation where only Bill's heart became the main event for nearly four years.

# GIFT OF THE LOST ARROW

Within the pages of my published journal, *Soul Sounds*, I'd mentioned that Sarah was interested in trying archery. Shortly after we moved into our Wildhorn house, Robin called me from work. One of her coworkers was an experienced archer and had read the book. She wanted to gift Sarah with one of her bows and some arrows that she makes herself. This lady also invited Sarah over to her rural home for the purpose of teaching her some basics.

Sarah was thrilled to hear of the kind offer and she gratefully accepted. My eyes widened at the sight of the large compound bow. Its pull was far too powerful for me when I tried it, yet Sarah persisted in her attempts to master the bow. And her determination paid off. Frequently she could be found out in the newly-created corral area aiming her arrows into her target attached to bales of hay, or else she'd be down in front of the house aiming toward a hillock.

One sunny day, when she was down in front of the house, she made a powerful pull on the bow and the arrow shot far off its mark. It shot far above the hillcrest to zing past its target and disappear into the deep forest. Her heart skipped a beat as her mind filled with fear. Had the errant arrow struck down a four-legged? Had it killed a brother or sister of the woods?

The bow dropped as she raced into the dense evergreens. She had to find that arrow. She *had* to find it.

Quickly, the search for the stray arrow began. Her forest-wise eyes scanned the undergrowth that was thick with budding wildflowers and shiny, newborn kinnikinnic. A movement caught her attention and she paused a moment to watch a lone coyote prance across a far, sun-lit clearing. Turning her attention back to the task at hand, her mind filled with thoughts of some innocent animal lying hurt and bleeding from her carelessness. Those heartbreaking thoughts brought her a panic that sent her frantically crashing through the forest.

Suddenly, there was the arrow; it had speared the trunk of a fallen tree. With a heavy sigh of relief, she bent to retrieve it, then sucked in her breath. Her sights were drawn to two curled shapes hiding among the bracken not five steps from the log. Her heart beat with building joy, for before her, sporting small white spots on their backs, were two small fawns.

Sarah was lost in the timeless moment of the special union before it was shattered by the terrifying thought that her arrow might have struck them. . .or struck down the doe! Tears welled within her eyes at that mournful thought. She remain crouched and sent loving thoughts surrounded by a warm, rosy light to the two forest babies. She spent several precious moments basking in the beautiful union she felt from the silent communication between them. Then, not wanting to distress the doe who was sure to be close by, she quietly backed away from the well-concealed hiding place. When she felt she'd put enough distance between them, she eased behind the wide trunk of a jack pine and peered her head around to watch a little longer. Her heart giggled to see the twin fawns, startled with the sudden sounds, shakily rise up on wobbly legs and totter off toward tall willows. Nosing out from the dense green twigs was the regal doe. Concerned and loving mother licked the head of each of her babies before the three turned to lock eyes with Sarah. Her heart soared as she watched them flick their ears. Her heart soared as her soul spoke softly to them.

"Thank you for being here in our woods. I would never harm you. Never again will I let my arrow fly through your home. I surround you in the light of my love. You are always welcome here. Here you'll always be safe."

And when the soundless spirit words were carried upon the breath of the gentle spring breeze, the three four-leggeds raised their heads to convey their understanding. Then they turned and slowly walked away.

Sarah stood in place to savor the magical encounter. She savored it and imprinted it upon her soul memory so she could call it back up from within her whenever she wanted. The archer tightly grasped the arrow and held it to her breast. To her breast she held it and whispered a Thanksgiving Prayer for its Gift. . .the gift of leading her to one of her most heart-welling and spirit-filled encounters. . .a woodland communication.

## GOODBYE COCAINE, HELLO RAIN

Around the beginning of August, I received a letter from a reader who'd previously sent me a beautifully beaded gift with No-Eyes' name worked into it. Tee wanted to personally meet with me for a few minutes in order to hand me another gift of appreciation that couldn't be sent through the mail.

Ordinarily I wouldn't have time for any more of these meetings with correspondents; in fact, I'd found it necessary to make that fact known through my last journal. Yet two circumstances prompted me to arrange this meeting with Tee. One was the need to get away from the house for a few hours. The other reason was that I was personally interested in meeting this young woman. Why? Because I wanted to praise *her*. I wanted to praise her for how she'd taken No-Eyes so completely into her heart that my teacher's presence there got her off cocaine. I was moved beyond words when she explained that to me in her letter. Tee had lived quite a life. She'd been a member of a motorcycle gang and had done it all. She was a tough cookie. She was currently hiding out from the D.A. when she wanted to meet. Could I not meet with someone who claimed that No-Eyes got her completely off a seven-hundred-dollar-a-day cocaine habit? This, to me, was one of the most spectacular and heartwarming effects I'd ever heard No-Eyes have on anyone. This young woman deserved a great big hug! So we arranged the meeting. The time and place was set.

I arrived at the Fossil Inn and sat in the lounge. I'd been waiting twenty minutes or so when the bartender shouted, "Is there a Summer Rain here?" I stood. There was a phone call for me. It was Tee. She explained that she didn't drive because a license plate could trace her. Her friend was driving her to the meeting point when their engine blew. We'd have to arrange another day to meet. We set it up for the following Sunday. Same time, same place.

The following week Sarah came with me. She too took advantage of opportunities that got her away from the house at that time. So she came with me when I drove the pickup down to the Fossil Inn. This time, I was barely out of the truck when my Biker Woman flew out the restaurant door and threw her arms around me. She and her two friends had been waiting for me this time.

The five of us crowded around a table in the lounge and Tee proceeded to tell me all about her life and how deeply I'd affected her.

I quickly corrected her. "You mean *No-Eyes* changed your life."

Our Tough Cookie frowned a mean frown. "No, Lady, *you* wrote those books. *You* changed my life."

"Tee," I insisted, "but I couldn't have written anything if it hadn't been for No-Eyes. It was *her* wisdom, *her* gentle life, *her* incredible abilities that gave life to the stories. It's all *her* doing."

This was not a good thing to say to someone who used to swing chains and shoot guns.

She made a mean face and put her fist under my chin. "*You* changed my life!"

"Right," I smiled, "but No-Eyes was still behind it."

She shook her head. "Why won't you believe it was you? If you're her messenger, then you have to stop denying that you had anything to do with how these books are working for people. You need an attitude adjustment."

We laughed at that. I didn't think I wanted Tee to adjust my attitude. We went around and around for a bit. She, insisting it was me. I kept insisting it was No-Eyes. I think Tee finally threw in the towel. . .probably because she didn't want to hurt me in order to change my mind.

Her friends too raved about how Tee was never seen to smile before the books changed her life. When I heard that, I looked to her and saw the most beautiful, full, and genuinely happy smile. "You've got great dimples," I grinned. "Your smile is beautiful." It nearly brought tears to my eyes to think this young woman never smiled, worse yet, that she never had anything to smile about. Now all I saw were her beaming smiles that radiated such inner joy and reflected her shining spirit.

Her friends told us about how she now lives with her grandma and that Tee even joined her aunt's Bible study group. Tee had wild tales to tell about that. It seemed that the Bible group consisted of ladies who got the biggest charge of having Tee participate. The ladies enjoyed her constant questioning and the metaphysical ideas that kept them in lively conversations—which usually ended up in verbal circle dances that they loved toestepping to. My visual of this was most amusing and brought a wide smile to my face.

The discussion then went around to what I'd been busy with and how we were doing in our new house. All I mentioned was that we had to have the entire house and garage painted because the wood was so dry. Tee was disappointed to hear that we'd had to pay someone to do that. "I could've gotten my biker friends to do the whole job for you!"

And that visual made me laugh. "Can't you just see dozens of bikers riding motorcycles up to my house."

She grinned. "Hey, we do good things. . .sometimes. Those guys would've been happy to paint your house."

"Ah, that's okay, Tee. The painter's already half done."

After about an hour had passed, we went outside to where our vehicles were parked. I moved the pickup over to hers. She didn't want anyone to see what she'd brought because we could get into some trouble if we were caught with them. Let it be known that her gifts were not drugs, weapons, or money.

I was so moved by her gifts, tears came to my eyes. I will treasure them always.

Tee's friends took pictures of us together with the gifts. I asked Tee if I could include one of these photos in my upcoming *Bittersweet* book and she graciously gave her permission.

I've since heard from her on occasion. She'd sent us a wedding invitation that I got the biggest kick over receiving. It was in the form of a Wanted Poster. At the bottom of it were these strong words of warning: NO DRUGS, GUNS OR ATTITUDES ALLOWED! Tee ended up marrying her long-time friend, Thunder. They are both Irish/Comanche and are happy residing in the Colorado mountains.

Tee is now doing great. She's free of all police troubles. She was cleared and has been off cocaine. She's busy helping others in recovery groups.

In my Prayer Smoke, I thank God for people like Tee. She's a real credit to the power of No-Eyes' sweet life and deep wisdom. Tee is a credit to the power of love. Tee is a credit to herself.

Incidently, I gave "Rain" the credit on this story's title. . .only so Tee won't be tempted to come give me one of her former-style "attitude adjustments." Ah, Tee? If you read this. . .I'm just kidding. I love you.

# A QUESTION OF VALOR

As mentioned earlier, we'd accepted a correspondent's generous offer of her horse. Valor was a young (very young) Morgan gelding that needed a good and loving home. His owner was relocating to another state and wouldn't have the room for him on her new property. We were excited about the wonderful gift and we worked like busy beavers preparing for the new family member.

Bill and Sarah worked long and hard to convert one of the garage bays into a fine stall. I even gave up our budget money that was supposed to go for carpet. . .which, instead, went for rubber mats to cover Valor's cement stall floor! I still can't believe we did that. Bill and Sarah also worked for weeks on fencing in a large corral that would give our equine plenty of space to roam and run.

Bales of green hay were stacked in the garage. A new plastic garbage can was filled to the brim with wonderful-smelling oats. A saddle perched on the workbench along with curry brushes, hoof scrapers and an array of other grooming equipment. Bill had cleverly devised a way to keep the wind and blowing snow out of the stall. He'd cut long strips of heavy-gauge vinyl that hung down over the stall opening. This horse was definitely going to be one pampered critter. All was ready and waiting just in time for his scheduled arrival from Florida.

The evening of Tuesday, August 17th, was a difficult one to get through. The hours crawled by. The clocks appeared to be moving more slowly than usual. Finally it was time for bed. The clock alarms were set for 4:00 A.M. because the big horse transport van was due to come up our drive at 4:30. I'm sure the rest of the family tossed and turned as much as I did. Who can soundly sleep with such high anticipation coursing through every fiber of their being?

Bill and I were up before the alarm sounded. The first thing I did was to turn on all the outside floodlights so the van driver could see us up on the hillside from Wildhorn Road. I then paced the deck listening for the approach of a large vehicle, watching in the dark for its headlights that I could see from our high vantage point. Finally the rattling sound was heard coming from the washboard dirt road. Then I spied the headlights round a bend. I ran inside. "He's here! Valor's here!"

The family sleepily pulled on warm coats to go out into the chilly, dew-covered morning darkness. We were all waiting by the stall when the van eased down our mountain drive and pulled up in front of us. From inside the van, loud stomping sounds were heard. We smiled at one another, eager to see the animal that seemed anxious to get out.

The driver introduced himself and made sure he was at the right place. Who in their right mind would be out at 4:30 standing in front of a stall unless they were waiting for a special delivery? The driver said that they'd been traveling with some mares that they'd just dropped off in the Springs. Valor had to be medicated because he was upset when the mares were off-loaded. And then we were jumping for joy when the men led Valor down the ramp and stood him before us.

Oh my! How *big* he was!

The handler led Valor through the corral gate and asked if we had a horse blanket. I went to get it and, when I came back, was embarrassed when the man said, "Better put it on 'im. He's not used to this chilly weather."

Huh? *Me* put the blanket on this huge animal? How did I tell this guy I didn't know which end was which? So I handed it to him. He smiled. "First horse?" And I grinned.

He'd glanced around. "Doesn't look like a 'first horse' set-up," he commented while blanketing Valor. "Looks like this fella's gonna live like a king." We were happy to have done things right. We were happy to have a good set-up for Valor.

Then the man handed me the halter lead. "Why don't you walk 'im around a bit—let 'im see what's what with his new home."

Huh? *Me* walk this monster around?

Sarah came up beside me. "Let's do it together, mom. I'll take one side, you hold onto the other." And that's what we did. We talked softly to Valor and eased him around a little. He seemed so calm and simple to lead.

We then brought him into the stall where he sniffed around a bit before going down on his knees, then lay in the fresh straw. His eyes drooped. His head kept nodding. Finally his nose rested on the straw and he dozed. Sarah lay beside him and stroked his side. She wanted to bond with him. She wanted them to form a special connection right off the bat.

Bill paid our half of the transportation costs and the van pulled away. The family stood and watched Valor rest, then we meandered back to the house.

That morning, after everyone was up for the day, we all were anxious to take a look at our new resident. Oh my, our sleepy-eyed and amenable newcomer was up prancing about the corral, kicking up his feet and loudly neighing for some of that luscious-smelling grub for breakfast.

Bill, Sarah, and I went out to the stall. Sarah rubbed his nose when Valor came over to her. Bill began pulling out handfuls of hay from the bales while I emptied some oats into an eating container.

I went into the stall and sat on the bench. I held the shallow container in my lap, and Valor pranced over to me and began munching with gusto. I laughed at a particular habit he had while eating the oats—he'd raise a front leg up and bounce it up and down as if to say, "Oh, oh, oh, this is sooo yummy!" Valor did this every time thereafter, but only with the oats.

Our first mistake with Valor was treating him like a pet that we could play with. Valor loved to run. . .hard. . .fast. Sarah, Mandy, and I would get into the corral with him and play chase. What absolute fools we were. What novices! Valor loved the game. We'd take off running and he'd stand there giving us a head start. When we were nearly half way across the corral, he'd take off at full speed, mane flying, and come charging past us to beat us to the fence line. Then he'd turn around and whinny as if to say, "You dumb humans can't outrun me! Ha! I won again!" And we'd go over to him and stroke his nose.

This game was foolish to start because Valor loved playing it so much. . .so much so that he thought we were going to play it whenever anyone walked into his corral space.

One sunny afternoon in early September, while Sarah and I were busy in the corral with shovel and wheelbarrow, she was over by the fence and I was walking toward the center of the corral. Before she could shout out a warning and before I could turn around after hearing the pounding hoofbeats fast approaching behind me, I was knocked down. I was hit hard. Just as I fell, a hoof nicked my head and I pulled in like a hedgehog. . .waiting. . .not moving. . .waiting for what was coming next. I wrapped my arms over my head and waited, thinking, "So this is how it ends." And I imagined Valor rearing up over me, ready to bring his hoofs down for the kill.

No sound came. There was no sound anywhere.

I slowly turned my head. I spied four hooves planted firmly, not two feet from my head. I looked up the legs. Valor was standing there, head down, looking at me. I uncurled. He looked puzzled. He looked sorry. . .like, "Oh oh, what'd I do?"

He turned his head as Sarah ran up to me. "Are you alright, mom? Oh, I was so scared! He just took off after you. He charged straight for you! I was so shocked I couldn't shout fast enough before he grazed you with his shoulder. Are you okay?"

I was rubbing my head. It hurt. "He nicked me with a hoof. I don't think he meant to. I don't think he meant to hurt me, he just wanted to play the race game with me." I looked at the animal. He was still standing there beside us. He seemed to be waiting for some sign that everything was okay.

I reached up and rubbed his nose. I don't know, maybe I should've scolded him or something, but I didn't think he'd know what it was for. And he watched us walk back to the fence and crawl through.

My injury was not severe, thank God. It only broke the skin and I felt bruised in several places. Other than that, no damage was done, other than some to our own prides. We then realized that you don't play with a horse and treat it like one treats a dog. Horses are powerful. Horses can do damage to one's body without even trying. Horses, for their sheer size and power alone, needed to be respected—and *trained.*

Valor had few vices. That, we learned, was what horse people termed bad habits. He didn't crib (nibble on the stall wood). He didn't rub on the wire fencing. He didn't do the really bad things that some horses are prone to do. But Valor did bite. Not "mean" bites, but just a lightning quick nip here and there. These could be slight nips as though they were a "just pretending" sort of statement or they could have much more jaw power behind them. Most of us had at least one spot on our skin that Valor left his teeth marks on. Those hurt when they came.

The experts told us to take our hand and whack him a good one on the nose or cheek whenever we got one of his nips. This was hard for us to do. Hit an animal? We're supposed to strike him? That seemed so out of character for any of us. Love and gentleness was how all our four-leggeds were always treated. How did one begin shifting a mind-set like that?

Sarah's school friend, who has been a horsewoman since she was old enough to toddle around, had once broken her arm disciplining her rodeo horse. Now that was *some* reprimand she gave her horse! In the end, I think our strikes were nothing more than love pats. We used sternness in our voices more than anything to get our message across to Valor. When we did that though, he'd raise his head and pull back his lips as if to be sassy and talk back, "You humans don't know anything about horses, I'll bite if I want."

Well, over those first few weeks, Valor did indeed teach us a lot about his kind. We learned respect. We also learned that *we* were supposed to be the boss—not him. And we all tried being more firm. Sometimes it worked. Sometimes it didn't. And because we were feeling our way with this, it took a couple of months before anyone felt ready to be up on this critter's back. Well, maybe the word "ready" doesn't quite fit. Maybe "brave" is more accurate.

Bill felt brave enough. He'd really been enjoying having Valor with us. He'd go over to him and call him Buddy. He'd talk and talk to him. Soon Valor sort of chose Bill as his favorite family member. He would nuzzle his neck and tease Bill by pulling off his hat with his teeth. I teased Bill back. "He only pulls your hat off so he can nip at the top of your head! He's no dummy." But we did notice how Valor nuzzled Bill more than the rest of us. Bill and his Buddy seemed to be getting on well. Bill and his Buddy appeared to be establishing a rapport. Bill was ready to ride his Buddy.

The morning was warm and clear. Bright blue skies looked down on the corral when Bill brought out the saddle blanket after brushing down Valor's back. He hefted the heavy saddle and Valor startled when it landed. I held onto the reins to keep him steady. Then Bill gave me an odd look. "Do you remember how all these straps go?"

Oh great. I didn't know anything about securing a saddle. He'd been the one to learn that.

I talked softly to Valor while he patiently waited for Bill to get it right. Now I think Valor was just pretending to wait. I think he was busy plotting.

Bill tested the tightness of the cinch. He checked and double-checked the straps. He looked at me. I felt a bit of anxiety from him. "Go for it," I prompted. "You'll never know unless you try it at least once."

He sighed. I think he too was feeling a little less brave at this point. He rubbed Valor's nose, then his side. He spoke softly to him, "Easy Buddy. Easy now." And he was sitting firmly in the saddle before I realized he'd done it. Yea!

Bill eased Valor out along the corral fence line. He wasn't ready to take him out in the open. He initially wanted to walk around the enclosed area.

Valor was behaving. Everything was progressing well. Bill was comfortable with it and went a little faster, then faster still. Valor was responding. Valor liked fast. Valor loved speed. Valor had a *need* for speed. Valor did a quick twist, a buck, and Bill was on the ground. In the blink of an eye it was all over.

I ran to him. He got up slowly, rubbing his side.

"I'm okay," he reassured. "I'm not hurt." Then he began looking around the ground for his sunglasses and hat. That was the end of riding for the day. . .I thought.

Bill walked over to the horse. He grabbed the reins and swung himself up again. His voice was stern. Valor's ears twitched around. Valor had not envisioned this second attempt in his plot.

Around and around they went again. They walked. They speeded up. They ran. Valor was wise enough to space out his little tricks. Valor was good.

Bill dismounted with a wide smile. "See? You just got to show them who's boss."

Right. Somehow I had the sinking feeling that it was Valor who really knew who the boss was. It was Valor who knew the score. It was Valor who was playing mind games with us by biding his sweet ole time.

A few days later, Bill rode again without incident. Sarah had been watching her dad. She was itching to ride. She sure loves horses. Watching her dad and seeing Valor on his best behavior gave her confidence. She wanted to try.

Once Sarah mounted, Bill first took the reins and walked her around on Valor. He wanted the animal to get used to the feel and sense of a new rider. Valor was good. Valor knew exactly what he was doing.

Bill then gave the reins to Sarah. She was in Seventh Heaven riding the horse around by herself. She began by walking him around the fence line and then eased into a trot, cutting across the corral. A steady gallop came next and her heart was filled with so much joy she was flying high. . .flying high and landing hard on the ground. I'd seen Valor do that little twist of his just before his back legs kicked up and his spine arched high. Sarah had been bucked off just the same way Bill had. We ran over to her. She was hurt, but escaped serious injury. For weeks afterward, her side and thigh bruises turned a rainbow of colors. She'd been badly bruised, but nothing major had been damaged. Sarah was never comfortable with Valor again, even though she did get back on him a couple of days later. . .just to allay the psychological effects of the experience.

One beautiful afternoon, when I was upstairs wallpapering our bedroom, I needed to retrieve something I'd left downstairs. Rounding the dining room corner, I stopped dead in my tracks. There, at the kitchen sink, was Aimee performing E.M.T. work on her dad's head. I rushed over. "What happened?"

They both grinned.

I nosed closer for a better look. Bill's forehead was bleeding profusely from a wide gash. My heart sunk. "What happened!"

He grinned again. "We were being quiet so you wouldn't hear."

Aimee was muffling a giggle.

"What didn't you want me to hear?"

Bill winced from Aimee's ministrations. "If you knew I was thrown again and saw the gash I got, you'd be scrubbing my skin off with steel wool!"

My mouth dropped. "You baby." Then I looked over at Aimee. "Did you debride it good enough?"

"Yes, mom. He's going to be fine."

I sighed. "You guys are never going to let me live that down, are you."

They both shook their heads. Bill didn't want me cleaning out his wound like I did for the girls when they were little and hurt themselves. I'd scrub and scrub that dirt out. They'd scream and scream while I did it, but it was clean and no infections ever set in because it *was* clean. If I felt their injury needed to be looked at, I'd run them up to the hospital emergency room and the doctors and nurses would never fail to comment on how nice and clean I got the wound. Bill didn't want anything to do with me cleaning out his.

I looked his injury over. It was bad. It was bad, yet not bad enough for stitches. Aimee had cleaned it, smeared antiseptic over it and was in the process of applying a butterfly bandage to keep it closed.

I gave them each a disgusted look. "Baby," I couldn't help adding beneath my breath before returning to my upstairs project.

So, Bill had been thrown twice. Sarah once. That was getting to be a real problem. None of us felt comfortable riding Valor. He was having his way with us. We were not experienced enough riders to anticipate a violent buck and hang on too. Valor was not ridden for a few weeks.

Then, one fall day was particularly beautiful. I'd been wanting the family to go for a walk in the woods and this was to be that day. Only. . .Bill insisted on riding Valor through the woods. Overall, it was a wonderful experience. We went up and down steep ravines which Valor took to like an experienced trail horse. We crossed streams. Bill ducked low-hanging branches. The only problematical incident came when I showed them the spot I was thinking about putting a rough cabin on. It was at a place where two deer trails crossed. Valor was not a happy camper there. He sensed something that was unsettling to him and his eyes began to roll. He started stomping and turning in circles. He began to rear. I urged Bill to dismount as fast as he could before Valor bolted. Bill would hear none of it. Instead, he got Valor out of there while talking softly to him and stroking his neck.

We're not sure what spooked Valor so badly. We don't think it was the deer scent because elk would come down out of the woods at night and bed down beside his corral. He wasn't real pleased with this at first, but he soon got accustomed to it and it never bothered him after that.

Sometimes though, at night when we were out taking care of him for the evening, we'd notice him suddenly look up into the woods. His ears would twitch and he'd begin to nervously prance about. It was obvious that something wild was up there. We didn't have a bear problem at this location. I hadn't had any contact with my cougar either, so we didn't think it had anything to do with that. We just weren't sure what he was sensing. Whatever it was, it scared him some nights. Many months later, in fact it was the following year, we did discover that a cougar had a den not far from our house and that our entire property was part of his range. As many times as I'd been out in those woods at night, I'd never once encountered him, nor did I ever hear his scream. . .until we were ready to move out the following year.

After Bill moved Valor out of range of my "cabin" spot, we continued into the woods for a long while. Finally the family was tiring and we headed home. Valor had been great. I was relieved to get him back into his corral without incident. However, my Pale Rider had other ideas. He wanted to take Valor out of the confining woods and to a place where he could run him full out. He went down the drive, turned Valor around, kicked at his sides and held on for dear life. Mane and tail flying, Valor raced up the long, curving drive. He ran so fast that I feared he'd run Bill right into the closed garage door. But Valor, being the clever one he was, turned five feet from the metal wall. Bill came to a full stop. Cheshire grin shining so proud.

"You scared me to death!" I cried. "He turned so fast you could've fallen off!"

Pale Rider had turned into a monster. He grinned. "Nah. That was fun! Wanna see us do it again?"

"*NO!*"

He and his trusty steed turned their backs on me. They acted deaf. Back they came like something out of the Apocalypse. Hooves thundering on the dirt. Mane flying. Bill laughing. Me closing my eyes.

I heard the hooves clamor on the cement pad of the garage. They'd gotten that close before Valor swung around to stop before me. I peeked around my fingers at them. What I saw were two bad boys. . .two very bad boys. . .both grinning at me. I turned and strode into the house.

We eventually had a horse trainer come out to evaluate Valor. Valor still didn't like people riding him unless he could speed our Pale Rider up out of the blazing fires of Hades. Valor's need for speed could not be tempered. He'd have none of the kiddie rides around the corral. He'd show his impatience with this baby stuff by doing his little twist and buck routine. We needed to do something.

The trainer thought Valor was a beautiful animal. He thought he only needed a refresher course because it'd been so long since he'd been ridden. Valor had been boarded too long. He'd forgotten a lot.

Well, we didn't have a penny extra to spend on horse training so we cared for Valor and loved him. He was treated like a king and given a lot of attention. Valor was not ridden again, though. He was too headstrong. He was too powerful to control when he got like that. We'd decided that we'd not give the dark side any opportunity to harm us. Valor was just such an option for them. While Valor lived in our corral, he never felt a saddle again. What Valor did feel, though, was lots and lots of love. Just because he needed training, that didn't keep us from heaping bushels and bushels of love and attention on him. It wasn't his fault he'd forgotten the rules. It wasn't our fault we were so inexperienced. So we both reached an impasse. The standoff was filled with love and, it was enough to keep us all happy and content for as long as need be.

Having a horse we couldn't ride didn't make that horse a useless animal, for we discovered that there were myriad other ways we could share a warm companionship with him.

Sarah would take a book out with her and perch comfortably on the concrete retaining wall that jutted out into the corral from Valor's stall. She'd sit in the sun and read, often taking breaks to softly talk to him. Valor's ears would flicker and he'd mosey over to her, nudge the book or her hair and pull those lips back in a great horse smile. Sometimes he'd be content to simply stand beside her. This was Sarah's way of being close to the horse she'd always wanted. This was her way of showing him how much she still loved him.

Bill. Now Bill had quirky little ways of interacting with the horse he had various names for. Sometimes he called him Buddy, other times he called him Butthead; either way, they were both terms of endearment, or so he claimed.

One of Bill's little fun things to do was to test Valor's perception of trust coming from Bill. This was nothing short of playing daredevil games as far as I was concerned, but he got quite a kick out of doing it. Actually, to be totally honest, it was all Valor's idea in the first place.

Bill would be working on repairing a portion of corral fence and he'd just be in a busy attitude that perhaps Valor interpreted as Bill ignoring him. Valor, never the one to like being ignored, would paw the ground to get Bill's attention. Bill would respond and turn to face the horse. The horse would then charge headlong straight for Bill and screech to a sliding halt in his face. Bill thought it was really funny how Valor came up with this "thing" he did. So. . .Bill turned the tables. Great idea. Just wonderful. Every time I saw him do this I sprouted twenty more grey hairs. Bill would walk into the corral and stand at one end. He'd call, "Hey, Butthead! Wanna test my trust in you again?"

Valor, sharp enough to recognize the call to play ball, would move into position, stare at Bill, snort and charge straight for him. Always. . .*always* stopping inches from Bill's nose. And my daredevil wouldn't even flinch. Never even blinked. Now *that's* trust. Maybe it was a lot more than that. Maybe it was a reckless kind of love.

Me? My quality time with Valor was "oat eat'n time" when he'd nuzzle my neck, do his little leg bobbing thing, pull my hair with his teeth, then run out in the corral and kick up his heels. What a ham he was. I loved him so much. Oh yes, he surely could be a royal Butthead, but most of all, most of all, he turned out to be everyone's Heart-Buddy. Oh yes, he certainly knew he'd wriggled his way into everyone's heart and he'd sometimes use that knowledge in odd little ways. He used it on me several times.

Once, when I'd been enjoying our quality oat eat'n time together, he tested the attention I was giving to the task at hand. In one flash, he'd flipped the oat container out of my hands. He must've had one good horse laugh seeing pieces of oats covering my hair and shoulders. It was the last laugh he'd had over that, though. From then on I was sure to give my grip on that container a lot of attention. He'd push his nose down on it hard, trying to make it fall. He'd suddenly grip the rim in his teeth and pull. He'd try every way he could to dislodge it from my hands. . .to no avail. You know? It got to the point where I could tell it was coming. I'd talk to him while watching him eat and bob his front leg. I'd sense his mood. And, sure enough, that playful mind of his would start planning his move. After awhile it got to be a game with me. Testing my awareness. Anticipating the moment he was going to make his move. It was great fun and I loved every minute of it.

Valor. Oh, Valor. What a character you were.

# DEATH COMES KNOCKING

On September 25th, Bill brought home a box of correspondence that Hampton Roads had forwarded to us. I never let these sit around for more than a day and liked to get to them as soon as they arrived.

When I saw the volume of mail, I dropped what I was doing and sat at my desk. This shipment was going to take the rest of the day to go through.

I was enjoying the letters. They helped to lift my mood. They made me feel appreciated and, during this problem time Bill and I were experiencing, they made me feel loved. Hundreds of people thought of us. They prayed for us. Just knowing this was a great blessing that I counted among my Thanksgiving Prayers each night.

One particular letter brought laughter to my heart and I was still smiling from it when I split open the next envelope. My smile vanished. Someone wanted to kill us.

I re-read the pages. Was this some cruel joke? Was it for real? Initially that's what I wanted to believe—that it was just some sick joke. Someone didn't like me and vented their feelings in a mean manner. By the time I'd read it four times, I realized that the letter had been sent by a really sick mind. Every member of our family was mentioned; no one was immune to this person's twisted plan. Finally, Bill, sitting across from me at his own desk, had his work disrupted by a change in my vibrations. He turned to me. "What's wrong?"

I raised a brow and handed the letter over to him. "Someone definitely doesn't like us," I said.

He read the letter over a couple of times before commenting. "This person's a little more than disgruntled. We'll make a copy for our file, then we're calling Gary." Gary Shoemaker was the sheriff.

Robin came through the office then.

Bill handed the letter to her.

Her face reddened when she read it. "This is sick! What kind of mind would even think of such things?" She looked at Bill. "You going to report this?"

He nodded. "I think we'd better. I'm going to call right now."

Gary wasn't in at the time, so Bill spoke to a deputy who happened to be the son of someone Bill knew. Bill knew an awful lot of people in the area.

The deputy came out to the house and sat at Bill's desk while he read it a few times. "How many of you handled this?"

We admitted that we all had.

"I'll take this back for evidence." Then he called the office and made an appointment for us to go in and do a taped interview with the sheriff, the undersheriff, and their detective. The appointment was scheduled for Thursday, October 1st, but first the deputy arranged for us to have an information-gathering meeting with the sheriff and undersheriff.

We went to this a few days later. The four of us sat in the station's conference room. We knew the sheriff, Gary Shoemaker, just from residing in the area for so many years. And the undersheriff, Nick Adamovich, was familiar with a few of my books because he was interested in the Native American culture. He'd spent time down in the New Mexico desert with some of the People.

They took turns asking the obvious questions. Did we have any known enemies? Had we received any sort of death-threat letters before? We responded with a No to each of those.

Did we suspect anyone in particular? That question brought a more detailed response. Yes, we did suspect someone who lived in the area, and we outlined our reasons. The two officers were not unfamiliar with this person. Our suspect was a self-proclaimed cult leader.

How did we account for the fact that the letter was posted out-of-state? Our suspect had friends who travelled in their job.

Could we correlate anything in the threat letter to anything the suspect had written in normal correspondence letters that I'd been receiving on a regular basis? Yes again. He heard voices. He acted on those voices.

Could we identify the handwriting as being the same. No. This, we pointed out, was because the writing was concealed. The two officers agreed. After they'd studied how the letter was composed, they also concluded that it had been stopped and started again many times; apparently, however, the writer wanted us to think it was all written at once. There were also mistakes made by the suspect that he didn't even know showed. These I can't reveal.

We talked a long while about this suspect. We were told what the sheriff's department knew of him. Overall, the information was not comforting. During this revealing conference, we learned of two more people connected with our suspect. One of these I'd received a letter from a few months prior.

After we concluded, we remained seated and began to chat about various subjects. Nick asked me if I knew of some obscure Apaches in southern New Mexico near the Mexico border. I responded. We spoke about my books and how public figures sadly become targets. We talked about Bill and me getting permits to carry guns. The sheriff admitted that, through the many years he'd been sheriff, he'd only granted a handful. He didn't see a problem with our situation, though. If we wanted to go through all the paperwork and weapon-qualifying red tape, he thought we were good candidates for such a permit. He did warn us that it'd only be good in Teller County. If we went down to Colorado Springs, we'd have a major problem. In the end, we decided against it. Regardless, I carried one anyway. I'd rather get in legal trouble than be dead.

I'm not sure how our conversation shifted to U.F.O.s, but it did. I began detailing the night the ball of light was pursued by the military helicopter when we lived in Holiday Hills. I was getting so excited all over again with the retelling that Bill chuckled and told me to settle down. I sighed and said I couldn't help it.

Gary and Nick were grinning.

I frowned. "What. You think I'm a nut case, I suppose."

They both shook their heads. Sheriff Shoemaker laughed.

"What I think is so funny is you're sitting here telling me this fantastic story without even knowing how many calls we got about it."

Now I grinned. "You got calls?"

He nodded.

"Then you know I'm telling the truth."

"Well a lot of people saw *something* that night."

I frowned again. "But this office is not confirming what those people saw."

"They saw *something* unusual."

I sighed. Again.

Nick grinned. "When I was down in the desert, every night I'd watch those skies. I want verification too." Then he recounted several odd incidents.

"When I worked at a sheriff's office in another state, one of our officers was driving behind an old model Chevy. The Chevy speeded up and so did the officer. The Chevy began to take off. Our officer took off after it. Our officer didn't realize the road was curving and he followed those car lights right off the road and onto the bumpy desert brush. He watched the taillights continue on in a straight line. . .*right up into the night.*"

"So," I said. "What kind of Chevy flies?"

Nick smiled. He just grinned and shrugged his shoulders.

"I didn't see it. It didn't happen to me."

Now I understood. He needed a personal encounter in order to believe.

Nick then recounted the time he'd investigated the call from a cattle rancher. His cattle had been mutilated. The carcasses had been carted off to a university department in Boulder. Nick wanted to have a better look at them. He knew what he'd seen and wanted to study it further. When he got to the university, he was denied access. He was told that animals had done it. He knew differently. Case closed.

We talked a few minutes more on the subject, then the sheriff had to leave for another appointment. We made arrangements to conduct the taped interview with the detective. We left.

On Thursday, we returned for the scheduled taping. I'd sat in the wrong chair and was asked to sit facing the camera. Oh great, another camera.

We were asked many of the same questions that Gary and Nick asked us during our initial conference. We were asked questions about our suspect. We were asked about our feelings.

"Are you fearful for your life?"

"We're uncomfortable and watchful now," I said.

"Do you believe this person can psychically harm you?"

I grinned at that. "No."

"Why?"

"Because only *he* believes he can do that. Only *he* thinks he's that powerful."

"And you don't?"

"No. He's only playing at being an adept. He's really only begun kindergarten."

"So you don't believe he can psychically harm you."

"No".

"You believe he can physically harm you?"

"No. Not him by himself. He's not capable of that, but he has followers who are. He has followers who would do whatever he told them to do. I'm uncomfortable with that."

"You believe his followers would harm you or your family if he told them to?"

"Yes. They believe he does great psychic feats."

"And you don't believe that?"

"No. I've caught him several times."

"Caught him? Would you explain that?"

"Yes. He claimed to know certain things about me through psychic means, but he was just pretending he psychically knew them because we'd discovered that someone had told him these things beforehand. I personally caught him in other areas of pretending psychic talents."

"Which were?"

"Pretending to psychically *see* how my house was laid out. He was totally wrong. He pretended to psychically visit me many times. He never did."

"How do you know this?"

"Because that's something I *would* know. And because, one time, I wasn't even home when he claimed to see me there. He's a believer in his own powers. He has none."

Bill too was asked a volley of questions about other aspects relating to our suspect. Bill was convinced as I was regarding the man's claims of power. And Bill also was concerned about this man's obvious ability to convince others of his Adept station.

The taped interview concluded. The sheriff's department would keep a watch on this person. They would try to get a handwriting analysis order. We had the death threat letter and several other letters this man had written us.

In the end, the handwriting analysis order was denied. We wondered what such an order took?

A few days later, we purchased handguns for the both of us. We got two apiece and began to wear one around the house. We went out on the property every night to feed and care for Valor. We had thick woods all around. We were not paranoid. We were cautious and wanted to be prepared.

A month later, another sick letter found its way to my desk. This one was from a different source and we again took it to the sheriff's office. This one was from a man out of state who said he was "going to come at me like Geronimo!" (The only reason I detailed this man's words is because of the special way this note was written. A copy-cat wouldn't know this way.) This second letter-writer had his name and return address on the envelope. This was probably his oversight, but it was clearly enough to trace him down. Our sheriff called the police department in this man's town and asked about him. Yes, they'd been watching him for other reasons and were just itching to get something on him. They'd watch him more closely. There was also something unique about this second letter which I'll omit for obvious reasons.

The third incident was not a death threat, but was so unusual that it was clear that it'd come from a less than sane mind. Someone was sending back my books with most of the texts black-lined and written all over. They called me a mean name and gave No-Eyes another derogatory one. These books also went to the sheriff's office. They wanted everything suspicious.

At the time this was transpiring, we were having our house repainted. The poor painter. He finished extra fast after we began wearing guns.

Wearing that gun on my hip was a real pain. It gave me a sense of comfort knowing I had something to reach for if need be, but it was a bother to always be strapping on and off. I hated it. I hated the fact that it was even needed. It hurt to know that we were hated. I hated Hate.

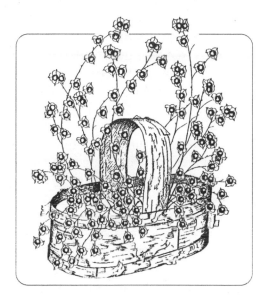

# BILL WELCOMES THE BAD GUYS

The death threat letters and other like correspondence put every family member on edge. We were more aware of our surroundings whenever we were out. We heightened our senses and were watchful. No one placed themselves in potentially compromising situations or was out alone at night. Routines were altered. Driving routes were varied. We had reason to change our telephone number. And, rather than be left alone during the day when Bill was gone, I had a safe place to go for a few hours. Nobody would leave me home without someone else being there. The door wasn't answered unless we knew who it was. The UPS man, Terry, thought it was a crying shame that I had to wear that gun. He began beeping when he came down the drive. . .just to ease my mind that it was him. He never said this, but I thought that was the obvious reason he started doing it.

When word got around about the death threats, friends began offering us an array of weapons to keep in the house. We didn't want to create an arsenal out of our home, yet every room had a weapon that could be reached for. We took the girls out and had them practice. They needed to know how to use them, experience the noise and feel of firing them. We practiced with all the handguns, rifles, shotguns, and others. We emptied rounds and gained speed in slapping new magazines in the .9mm and dropping quick-loads into the revolvers. Then we backed away from it. Practice over, we tried to maintain a normal day-to-day existence. That wasn't as easy as we would've liked it to be, for the fact that we may have to defend ourselves at any point in time was never far from our minds.

What was satisfying for me personally was that nobody got paranoid over this thing. We didn't get suspicious of people around us when we were out. We didn't think a delivery person was a killer coming to the door. We weren't afraid of the night. We didn't jump at shadows. Considering the wording of that first death threat letter, we should've been shaking in our boots. We weren't. We were confident of our protection and we only took precautionary measures to defend ourselves if the need arose. Each day was a little more relaxed than the previous one.

Then an amusing incident happened one night when Bill, Sarah, and I were out taking care of Valor. Well, it was amusing after the fact, of course.

Saturday night, November 28th, Sarah was in the garage bay grabbing bunches of hay to take out into the corral. Bill was back by the opened bay door. He had his rifle in his hand and he was just coming out of the garage. I was standing along the fence holding Valor's oat container. Valor was busy chomping and trying to flip his bowl on me.

The night was very cold. It was clear. Stars twinkled down. The three sets of bright floodlights on the garage were shining out in all directions. We were well lit.

Suddenly Valor whipped his head up. His ears twitched as he stared up the drive.

I looked up into the darkness at the top of the rise. I heard an engine. A vehicle nosed over the hill. It stopped.

I looked up at the glaring eyes of the headlights that were beaming down on us. "That must be *Jim," I said. I was referring to our neighbor friend next door. He went back to his home in Colorado Springs on the weekends.

Bill had wanted to tell Jim something. He raised the arm with the rifle and, with his other hand, waved the car down.

"*C'mon!*" he shouted.

The car idled at the top of the rise.

Bill shouted again. "C'mon *down!*"

The car didn't move. It just idled, twin headlights beaming down on us.

Subconsciously, I balanced Valor's bowl on my knee and moved my right hand to my hip, pulling my jacket back away from the .357 Magnum that perched there.

Again Bill waved the rifle and called to the driver of the idling vehicle.

Finally the engine was gunned. The vehicle spun its tires and turned around at the top of the drive. We heard it speed back down to the road.

Bill, Sarah, and I looked at one another. We wondered why our friend didn't come down the drive. Not two minutes later, I was still pondering the incident while glancing up the empty drive when something caught my eye. Our neighbor's lights had just gone out. Who was in his house?

"Bill! Jim's house lights just went out. Someone's in his house!"

Bill raced up the drive.

Soon I heard him talking to someone. He and Jim then appeared on the rise. They were walking down toward Sarah and me.

"Jim's just leaving *now*," Bill said. "He was in the house all the time. That vehicle wasn't him."

Because the vehicle's headlights were shining down in our eyes and all was blackness behind them, we never were able to make out the kind of vehicle it was. We'd thought it was our neighbor's car at the time because absolutely nobody ever turned up our private road. So naturally we assumed it was Jim leaving to go out to dinner or back to the Springs.

Jim was disturbed by the incident. He knew of our death threats and had been one of those offering us the use of a weapon. He was deeply concerned about this strange vehicle that idled at the top of our drive.

"Did you see the make?" he asked me.

"I can't tell one from the other," I admitted. "But when it turned, I could see that it was a light color. It looked beige."

"Could you see anyone inside?"

"The headlights were too bright to see past them. When it finally backed up and the beams weren't in my face anymore, I thought I saw three men."

Jim was not happy.

Neither was Bill.

There was nothing we could do about it now. The vehicle had sped back down our mountain without us realizing that we should've cut it off at the ravine in front of our house. We could've at least seen what make it was.

The incident was disturbing, especially since all of us inherently knew there were guys inside that vehicle with bad intentions.

What had changed their minds?

It was then when the incident became amusing. We recalled how Bill had held up his rifle and *invited* the vehicle to come down. I remembered checking my gun. Why I did that I didn't know until now. Something made me expose the weapon that headlight beams illumined. The men in that vehicle must've been thrown into confusion to see us standing at the bottom of the drive, guns exposed, welcoming them to come down to us. I don't imagine they ever expected to come upon a scene like that one. And we laughed and laughed over it for days afterward.

It was such an innocent invitation Bill gave to that car. Here we were, thinking it was our neighbor and waving and calling to him. Here we were, inviting the bad guys to come see us. . .waving Guns of Invitation. I can't imagine why they didn't want to go through with their visit. Maybe because it looked more like an ambush than an invitation to tea.

Although we laughed about the incident, the humor of the situation's little twist of fate didn't negate the fact that it had been serious. The humor didn't prevent us from realizing that the outcome could've been far more serious if we hadn't reacted the way we did. It had served to confuse the passengers of that vehicle. It had served to defend us in an unconventional manner. Our own misinterpretation of that vehicle was what thwarted probable injury or death that night. Sometimes, sometimes, one's defense comes in the guise of innocence. And for our visitors, that innocence was perceived as a challenge. . .an armed challenge.

This incident happened nearly three months after receiving the first death threat letter. We hadn't let our guard down. We were thankful that we still took weapons out to do the corral chores each night. We were thankful that we hadn't gotten complacent. We'd been innocent that night. We'd been innocent, but still ready.

During the days following this event, visuals of a Trail Marker kept spearing across my mind's eye. I'd previously had a vision of this object come clearly into my Vision Way Smoke. I knew it was something I was being urged to make. I knew it involved protection. . .protection of a very different kind. Now I was not going to put the creation of this Spirit Guardian off one more day.

Bill went down to the saw mill in Florissant and brought home a tall pole. He secured it in the ground alongside our drive down near the entry gate. Upon it he hung what I'd made. . .a steer skull with black painted around its eye holes. On each outstretched horn I hung three long strands of horse hair. Beneath the skull, on a horizontal pole, swung seven buffalo rib bones. Centering these was a medicine bundle with certain items inside.

The black eye holes stared out.

The long hair strands eerily swung in the breeze.

The seven bones clanked in the wind.

Now I knew we were really safe.

# PALE RIDER MEETS THE DOG CATCHER

Thanksgiving had come and gone. December was upon us and anticipation of the holiday season was not high. This had not been a good year for celebrations of any kind, yet each morning all family members urged themselves to greet the others with a smile and make personal efforts to glean something worthwhile from the waking hours before day's end.

Bill, too, made efforts to break the long cycle of darkness that had shadowed our lives during this time. On Thursday, December 10th, he'd come up with a winner.

Our next door neighbor friend, Jim, was single and lived alone; however, he was anxiously expecting his brother *Willie that evening. Willie and his lady friend were relocating here in Colorado from California. They would be pulling past our gate sometime that night.

Bill had ingeniously planned an unusual reception for the Colorado-bound couple. He had devised quite a Western Reception. Sarah thought it was ridiculously funny. Jenny wasn't sure, and I just shook my head. Oh yes, I did think the idea was an amusing one, but some nebulous thought lingered in the back of my mind that I couldn't quite bring to the forefront.

Around the time dusk settled in, I watched Bill don his long black western duster. He stood before the mirror and set the black hat with the string ties on his head. Pulling on his black gloves, he reached for the crowning touch. . .his rifle. The California pair were going to get a true western welcome from none other than Pale Rider in the flesh.

Bill turned to face me.

I was impressed. In the dark of night, he'd cause Eastwood himself to flinch at first sight of him. He'd done a great job with the effects. So far, so good, and I watched him stride out the door.

Sarah was excited to see how this little plan was going to work. She rode down in the van with the tough-looking gunman and they waited down by the gate for their guests to pull up. They were watching for two cars. Willie was going to be following his brother up to the house.

From the hilltop location of our house, I could stand in an area that gave a glimpse of the road down below between a few tall pines. I pulled on a jacket and went out to watch the action from above. I waited and waited.

Finally I saw a vehicle pass our gate. I heard brakes and its tires slide on the gravel. Taillights lit up. The vehicle was backing up. What was going on? I wondered. Then I heard other vehicles pull up and voices rose up on the breeze. I waited and waited to hear laughter. None came. The whole thing didn't feel right.

I went inside to get a warmer coat. I intended to walk down the drive to see what happened when headlights came around the rise by the house. Bill and Sarah pulled up.

"Oh mom!" she exclaimed, jumping out of the van, "you'll never guess what!"

"Probably not," I said, "what happened down there?"

"Go over to Jim's, they're unloading Willie's stuff already.

Frank came over too. He'd heard the sheriff's transmission over his scanner."

Sheriff's transmission? Frank was here too?

Frank Gonzalez was a close friend of ours. Our meeting was detailed in *Soul Sounds*.

I ran next door and heard laughter and joking going on as the group busied themselves moving boxes from car to house.

"What happened?" I anxiously asked.

Everyone laughed.

Bill was given the honors. "Well, Sarah and I were sitting down at the gate in the van to keep warm. We waited and waited for Jim and Willie. I wanted to stretch, so I got out and set the rifle up against the truck. A vehicle went by. It was the sheriff's animal patrol guys who live up the road. They'd spotted the rifle and how I was dressed. They didn't like what they saw and skidded to a stop. Just then, Jim and Willie pulled up."

"Oh no!" I grinned. This was getting funny.

"Yeah," Bill laughed. "There we were, the sheriff's dog catchers were looking at all our licenses and calling them in. They'd given their location which Frank heard over his scanner. He came right over to see if we were okay.

"Jim kept trying his darndest to convince them he was a doctor and lived at the top of the drive, but he couldn't find one piece of identification on him that proved his profession. He couldn't believe it. Then one of the deputies went over to the van and asked Sarah who she was. She told them that she was 'that guy's' daughter, pointing to me, and that we lived up the drive too. She said we were just playing a joke on our neighbor friend."

I was laughing hard by this time. What a messed-up joke this had turned out to be.

Bill went on to conclude the story. "So the dog catchers with their guns finally believed us and we began chatting. I told them about you being a writer and the death threats you'd received. I informed them that Gary and Nick were our friends and knew of the incidents."

I was upset after Bill had reminded me about that issue. "Well, if Nick said he was going to have his deputies keep an eye open for us, how come these guys who drive right by our road twice a day didn't even know about it?"

Bill shrugged. "I don't know. They knew nothing about the report we made." He grinned then. "One thing they *were* sure of though."

"What?"

"They said that it was a good thing they hadn't known about our report of the death threats. If they *had*, they said they probably would've come at us with guns drawn and asked questions later. . .much later at the station!"

I giggled with the visual of that.

"You think that's funny?" Bill asked.

"Well isn't it? Your timing with this little prank was just perfect!"

"Perfect for what?"

"For *real* out-west deputies to greet Willie!"

He frowned. "What about me? My whole plan got wrecked. Nothing went according to plan."

I smiled and kissed him. "You still got a good laugh out of it, didn't you? How often does Pale Rider get brought down by the dog catchers?"

That brought another burst of laughter by everyone in the garage. Everyone was laughing. . .even Bill. And it sounded like music to my ears.

Bill's foiled prank was talked about and chuckled over for weeks to come. It provided us with some gaiety to break up the problems that continued to plague those within the Changeling House. My Pale Rider had inadvertently brought some laughter back. He had brought a little sanity into a very crazy time.

# 1993

# THE MAGIC IS GONE

The holiday season of 1992 came and went without heartfelt celebrations from any of us. We allowed it to pass and made valiant attempts to forget about it. The new year was here and that meant new experiences and, more importantly, new beginnings that left old endings behind us. We *hoped* new beginnings were in our future.

January began on an even keel. There were no drastic highs or lows to go through. We managed to keep the flow of life at a manageable level.

On the evening of the 18th, Bill and I were in my native room. We'd just made up some snacking sandwiches and were preparing to watch a movie on television together. Robin appeared in the doorway.

"A woman just came to my door downstairs and said she

thinks she hit our dog. Is Magic in here with you?"

My heart stopped. "She's out in the woods."

Bill jumped out of his chair. "We'd better go check." He then grabbed his gun.

That reaction surprised me. "You don't think this is some trick to get us down by the road, do you? Are you suspicious?"

"No. I don't think this is any trick like that, but if Magic's in a bad way, we need to end her pain. This is just a precaution."

Bill and I took the van down to our gate where we saw the woman's car sitting in the road with her headlights shining on the still form of a white and honey-colored dog.

It was Magic. She had been thrown off by the side of the road beside the tall willows.

Bill immediately went over to her to check her injuries. Robin was already checking her out.

I hugged the woman who was beside herself with grief over what she'd done. She was crying about how it happened. "The dog just darted in front of my headlights. Oh God!" She cried great tears. "I could *hear* the bones snapping! I'm so sorry! Oh, I'm so sorry!"

I held her. "You can't control what happens when you're driving down these dark roads. Animals dart out in front of cars all the time. We almost got a stray elk once. You just can't blame yourself when this happens. She shouldn't have been down by the road. She wasn't allowed down here. It's not your fault. Please. Please don't blame yourself."

Finally the woman eased herself back into the car and it slowly passed us.

I went over and knelt down beside the group in the van's light beams. "What do you think?" I asked Bill while stroking Magic's battered little body.

"I don't see anything major, but there's obviously internal damage done."

I cooed softly to Magic. It pained me to see her scraped legs and face. I wondered if whatever was damaged could be repaired before it caused further injury. Could we get her to the vet's in time? Should we end her pain right now? I looked up to Bill's face. "What do you think we should do?"

He looked to Robin. "Open up the van doors. Mary and I'll

try to act as a stretcher and get Magic inside. We'll call Joel when we get back up to the house."

Joel was not available. This was his night working as attending veterinarian at the Animal Emergency Center down in Colorado Springs. We were to bring Magic right down where he could take some x-rays and see what he could do for her.

We didn't like to hear this. We didn't like it at all. The drive down to Colorado Springs from our Wildhorn Road house would take about an hour. We felt we didn't have an hour to waste. Magic had been whimpering. Each mournful whimper stabbed at our hearts.

Bill and I ran out to the van. We were going to go for it. The girls came with us. Nobody wanted to be parted from our hurt little family member. Aimee and Sarah sat in the back so they could keep her covered and watch her breathing. Mostly, they needed to be close to her and give loving comfort.

We made it to the Emergency Center in record time. Joel was ready for us and came out with a small stretcher. Just seeing the tiny portable bed was heart-breaking.

After the x-rays were taken, we were told that she had multiple fractures. The most serious was the hip.

We studied the films while discussing our options. Joel was Magic's vet. He knew her history. She'd recently developed arthritis and had thyroid problems which we gave her medication for. Our bottom-line question at this point was: What was Joel's professional opinion of Magic's quality of life if we went through with surgery?

It was decided that we'd have her operated on. Joel set it up with the best animal surgeon in the city. Joel would transfer Magic to the surgery center when he got off duty in the morning.

Our drive back up the pass that night was a quiet one. All of us were lost in personal thoughts and many prayers for our little four-legged friend.

On Thursday, January 21st, Magic went into surgery. The call we received was encouraging; she'd done well. She'd need a couple days with them so they could monitor her progress.

When I called to check on Magic's status on Saturday, I became concerned. She was not doing as well as expected. She was very depressed and not eating.

I asked the doctor if perhaps she just missed her family and maybe she'd recuperate quicker if she was at home with us. Well, yes, he thought that might be the best for her.

So we dropped what we were doing and went down to bring our baby home. We knew how much she missed us. We knew she'd be on her way to a speedy recovery if she had us around her.

When we got to the center, we were led back to the indoor pens. Magic was sprawled out on the floor of the last one. We went inside and knelt down beside her. The tip of her tail waved a little when she saw us.

The center's assistants gave her a bath and dried her off. We carried her out to the van and made her comfortable. We drove home with the wonderful feeling that our family was complete again.

Robin had offered up her living room for Magic's recuperation area since it was too difficult for Magic to manage stairs to go outside. We'd made a soft bed for her and placed her bowls near her head. Whenever she needed to go outside, we had to make a stomach sling out of a bath towel and lift the weight off her legs so she could walk and exercise the bones.

That evening, I slept on the couch and stroked Magic's side as she rested on the floor beside me. I got her to eat a little, but then she wouldn't keep it down. I encouraged her to lick a small amount of food off my hand and she managed to retain that. I wet her lips and urged her to drink a bit. During that night I helped her outside three times.

In the morning, she seemed to be in a great deal of pain. Bill placed a call to Joel who came out and looked at her. He ended up giving her something to make her more comfortable.

Shortly after our vet left, while Sarah, Jenny, and I were sitting next to Magic, I noticed that she began to pant. I wondered if we were crowding her and making her too warm. Rather than any of us moving away from her, I lifted her blanket off.

The panting didn't ease.

Aimee had left to go into Woodland Park for a prescription Joel wrote out for Magic. Bill was upstairs in our office attending to some phone calls. Jenny, Sarah, and I kept watch over our baby.

Suddenly Magic scared me. She got up on her front legs and turned over. What sickened me was the position of her injured leg—it was bent back beneath her in an impossible position. She acted like she couldn't even feel it.

I lifted her up and repositioned her leg out where it belonged and became increasingly concerned that she'd not felt what should've caused unbearable pain.

The panting continued.

I lowered my face to hers. "She shouldn't be panting like this," I whispered to the girls.

"She's just warm, mom," Sarah assured.

"No, I don't think that's it. I think something's wrong."

Sarah refused to believe anything could be wrong. "Mom, you're too worried about her. She'll be fine."

And we sat in silence while stroking Magic's soft fur and whispering sweet words of love into her ear.

Watching her the way I was made me aware of a change in Magic's breathing. She'd pause a little longer than usual between breaths. I bent again. I looked close at her eyes. They didn't notice me. My heart lunged.

I didn't want the girls to know what I was testing, so I nonchalantly passed my hand over Magic's eyes in an innocent move to pet her. She never blinked or made any indication that she'd seen my hand coming to her eyes.

My heart stopped as an icy chill shot up my back. "Oh my God."

The girls came to attention. Sarah looked up at me. "What!"

"Magic isn't seeing like she should."

"Oh mom, she's just sleepy."

"Sarah! Magic has her eyes wide open! Look! When I shade them the pupils don't change!" I'd passed my hand in front of the dog's eyes. Light or dark, they were fixed and dilated.

Then I knew.

"Oh GOD! Magic's DYING!"

Sarah refused to believe it.

Jenny began sobbing.

"Quick," I said, "let's turn her over. Maybe she needs to be on her other side."

We turned our baby.

Still she panted between slow breaths.

Still her eyes were fixed and dilated.

Still her breathing slowed and slowed.

And she twitched.

"See?" Sarah said, "she's moving. She's okay."

"That was a death shudder! Hurry! We can try C.P.R."

And we did. We tried and tried. I did the compressions while Sarah breathed into Magic's mouth. We kept it up but. . .Magic was gone.

All the tears we'd been saving up for months came flooding out of our eyes. We cried. We sobbed. We talked to our baby. We lay over her still body and dug our fingers into her fur.

Bill came downstairs.

I looked up to him. "Magic's dead," I cried. "She's *gone!*"

His reaction was one of total defeat. "It's so unfair," he said. "It's so unfair." And he walked over to the phone to call Joel.

"Joel? Magic just died. Can you come and take her aw. . ."

"No!" I shouted at him. "Nobody's taking Magic anywhere! We'll keep her here. We'll bury her right here."

It was a mournful scene that Aimee walked into when she came happily running down the stairs with Magic's prescription in hand. She froze. Tears trickled down her eyes. She just stood frozen in place. "She can't be dead. That's not fair. All we've been through and *They* take her away." Aimee turned and went back upstairs and closed her bedroom door to mourn in private.

Joel returned to the house for the second time that day. He was so sympathetic. He sat on Robin's couch in silence as he watched each of us bend over Magic and speak our final words to her. I never dreamed that I could display such emotion in front of someone, but I kissed and hugged our baby. I cried my eyes out while I told her what a great watchdog she'd been for us—she was the *greatest!* I told her how much I loved her. I bent to her face and whispered that she meant the world to me and she'd always have a warm place to live in my heart. I talked and stroked and hugged. Then I gave her a final gentle kiss on the head before getting up and going upstairs to join Aimee.

Sarah and Jenny had their turns saying goodbye to our tiniest and kindest family member. They too released all their emotions as they hugged and kissed. They too joined Aimee and me upstairs.

Bill and Joel discussed the situation. Joel offered to have an autopsy done on Magic if we wanted a document as to cause of death. Bill declined and accepted Joel's explanation— she'd had a massive pulmonary embolism.

Joel hung around to help bury Magic. Bill had arranged for someone to come over with a backhoe. The ground was too frozen for us to hand dig any grave deep enough to keep predators away.

The grave was dug.

Bill and Sarah carried Magic to the site.

We silently stood and cried as the grave was covered over.

We remained for a long while.

We felt a great hole in our hearts.

We knew our lives would be more empty now. . .now that the Magic was gone.

The following day, a small marker appeared at the head of the little hilltop mound. Nothing was etched upon its surface— nothing had to be, for there were no words to put there. It remained blank and empty. . .just like our hearts.

A week later, flowers were in front of the marker. Each of us had made separate and private visits to talk to Magic. And, we discovered, though we'd never hear her bark again and we'd never feel her lick away our tears. . .Magic still lived. We had sweet and wonderful memories. It was the emotions those memories stirred that made our baby immortal.

# ASSASSINS IN MY SMOKE

One February evening, when the snow was gently falling outside and all was still and quiet in the house, I was preparing to begin my Prayer Smoke. It was quite late at night and everyone had been abed long ago. This created the perfect atmosphere for the solitude I required. Midway through preparations, I froze. Something bad speared my consciousness. Some bad thing had entered my field of protection.

Not knowing the source of this intruder, I quickly put away my articles and turned out the native room lights. I peered out the sliding glass doors. I saw nothing. It was what I *felt* that prickled my spine incessantly. WARNING! WARNING! DANGER APPROACHING! DANGER APPROACHING!

These were the words that screamed through my awareness. Warnings of what? I wondered. Danger from what? Who?

I don't know why I never broadcast the warning signal to the other family members. I don't know what made me sit in my reading chair, gun in hand, and watch out the sliding door blinds. I knew nobody could see me sitting there, but I sure could see anyone coming around the corner of that deck. The moon was bright. I didn't have to turn the floodlights on. I preferred it that way.

I sat for three hours holding that gun and watching. I sat for three hours listening. I sat for three hours waiting.

Suddenly the defensive attitude vanished. It was as if a great shield had lowered. It was no longer needed. I actually felt a sharper clarity of atmosphere between me and the door as if *something* had left the space.

I set the gun on my chairside table and thought about what had just transpired. What had been such a viable threat that I'd been forced to take a defensive stance? What had been approaching? What had just happened?

There was no way I could obtain these answers without some extra help. I lit a fire in the fireplace and sat before it. I offered my Thanksgiving Prayers in preparing my inner state for receiving a vision. I then requested understanding of the recent event and clarity of facts.

I watched the smoke.

Within it appeared the form of the Trail Marker I'd made several months earlier.

Our gate down by the road materialized.

A car moved through the gate. A beige car. A beige car with three men inside.

The car crept over the stream and eased up to the Marker. It stopped.

Suddenly the vision telescoped and it was as if I was standing next to the opened window of the car. I felt like I was in spirit and watching an event unfold.

The driver stopped the car. "What the hell. What's that!"

The passenger shrugged. "Looks like some native mumbo-jumbo thing. Got me. Let's get going and get this over with."

"No!" came the order from the back seat. "I *seen* them things before. Out on some reservations there's things just like that."

"Yeah?" said the passenger, "so what?"

The man in the back leaned forward to squint through the windshield.

The three looked at the object lit up by their headlamps.

The stark white skull stood out in all its power. The black eyeholes stared at the men. The six long black hairstrands swung in the breeze. The hanging bones clanked.

The driver shivered. "Oh c'mon, you guys gonna let some nutty thing like that scare you?"

The passenger wasn't sure.

The man in the back was sure. "You don't even know what that is, do you, you dumb-shit. That's a *Ghost* Marker! Man, like that thing's *alive*! They put those out to guard the trail against people who shouldn't be going up it. They got some kinda spirit energy attached to it. Hey! I don't care what you two wanna do but I'm not crossing that thing. I heard about people who didn't believe in them. I'm outta here right now." And the man in the back reached for the door handle.

"Wait a minute! No shit? You really believe that thing's got some power?"

"I *said* I seen 'em before, didn't I? I *said* I heard they work! I *said* I'm outta here!" And again he reached for the handle.

The vehicle lurched in reverse and tires spun. The three men were on their way back down Wildhorn Road, never to return again.

I'd heard their mumblings as they pulled away from me. "We don't need this. This whole thing was a bad idea from the beginning. We don't need to do other people's dirty work. Let's go."

The smoke cleared of all images and my message had concluded. So that was it. So that was why I'd taken the defensive stance and waited. I'd waited for these three guys to come do their dirty work. And I realized that their vehicle had been the same car that had idled at the top of our drive the night Bill waved them down. That gave me an icy chill. So they *were* assassins that night. So assassins *were* down at our gate tonight. Except this time, this time the Ghost Marker had been well established along the drive.

I sat before the fire and contemplated all I'd been shown. I believed in the power that had been given the Marker, yet there was some tiny aspect of me that wondered how such a thing could truly be effective against one's attackers. Now I had my answer. Now I knew how powerful it was. Now I knew it was a true Ghost Marker.

These thoughts led to other related ideas and ponderings. I couldn't begin to speculate on *what would've happened if the Marker hadn't been in place.* I was intensely curious about that and thought perhaps my Smoke would be kind enough to provide me with an answer.

Again I whispered the Thanksgiving Prayers. Again I added the cedar to the fire embers. Again I waited.

This time new images formed within the rising smoke. This time the beige car paid no attention to the Ghost Trail Marker and continued to snake up our hillside drive. Reaching the crest, headlights were turned off.

The scene altered.

The three men burst through our front door. I aimed the gun I'd been holding while waiting for them. I managed to down one man as he entered.

Bill, hearing the commotion downstairs, came out of the upstairs bedroom with gun in hand and shot down at the two others who were coming through. One went down. Two went down. Yet the second didn't fall until he too had gotten off a hit. Bill tumbled down the stairs. The hit had been a fatal one.

If the Marker hadn't halted the assassins that night, four people would've been dead, three killers. . .and Bill. This last vision of a failed probability made my heart shudder. I erased the insidious images from my mind and focused on offering up prayers of Thanksgiving that were more intensely heartfelt than anything I've ever sent up prayers for.

When I relayed the information to the family the following morning, they were filled with an array of mixed feelings. Some were angered that I hadn't awakened them. Some felt bad that I'd sat for three hours waiting for "something" bad to appear. Bill was amazed that nobody else in the family perceived the approach of such a dangerous and possibly fatal situation. We all were surprised that the outcome would've taken away one of our family members if the second scenario had taken place.

For days afterward, we gave more attention to aspects of maintaining our safety. Then, as before, the incident faded and ended up merely simmering on the back burners of everyone's mind.

Our lives were in jeopardy. That fact couldn't be denied. What puzzles us—to this very day—is the why.

# LOVE ME, LOVE ME NOT

My little four-legged companion, Magic, was taken from us on a Sunday morning. That evening, Bill offered to gift Valor to our vet. Joel had always wanted a Morgan. He'd planned on having a Morgan to go with the small carriage he'd envisioned taking him through the mountain roads for his veterinary calls. After some hesitation, Joel accepted Bill's gift. The following Saturday, Bill led Valor out to the horse trailer Joel had brought down to our stall. It was a sad day for everyone.

The family found various means of occupying their time in order to get their minds off our recent losses. I found that delving into the stacks of readership mail that had piled up did just that for me.

The first one I opened was from a correspondent who was

extremely upset when he received an AIM (American Indian Movement) Newsletter in which listed those individuals who the organization viewed as "plastic Indians." These represented people who were speakers, teachers, lecturers, authors, and other public personalities who addressed Native American issues without having been sanctioned by a Council of Elders placing their stamp of approval on them. Of course, Mary Summer Rain was among those listed. In a nutshell, all the names were being blacklisted by AIM. And my correspondent was outraged.

As I scanned the very lengthy list of names, I was upset to see Sun Bear's name among the others. Did AIM not have respect for the dead? How was it they could choose those who could speak, and pass judgment so freely on all others?

Many of the other names listed were truly famous authors and speakers. I was peanuts compared to them. What deeply concerned me was that they were grouping these people under the title of teachers. I am not a teacher. I don't go out and teach lessons or ceremonies. I don't speak of native ways. I don't conduct seminars. I'm not anything other than a person who wrote of her personal experiences. I guess I can't do that. According to AIM I need a Council Elder's express permission to write of my life and what I've learned from its experiences. I think AIM is somehow transposing my own teacher's native heritage to me. That is a big mistake. Besides, *no council here on earth holds the copyright on spiritual truths.* Gosh, that's like saying that only the Pope can write of Catholic spiritual experiences. Well, no matter, I'm done being concerned about what people think or say. I've passed that stage long ago. I'm nearly done here, so most of the words have already been said. I came and did what I was given to do—more is not required of me.

The above letter was not a great one to comfort me while making an effort to lift myself up out of my raw grief. The second one I opened was from the Albuquerque Native American Cultural Center. They were requesting an appearance and book signing. What? It appeared that, according to the Center's representative, I had many loyal readers in their area and requests were frequently made to have me visit the region for an autographing. This lifted my spirits before dashing them again with the thought of AIM members picketing the Cultural Center if I went.

Love.

Hate.

I responded to the invitation with a soft refusal. I declined with respect. I couldn't go where I may not be wanted and I'd never place myself in a position where I could cause discord. I've never asserted myself in a native manner. I've never had the inclination to participate in any native cultural events. . .just for the simple reason that some may think I don't belong there. Therefore, why go? I'm completely comfortable with this position, for I'm not here for the native people, I'm here for *everyone*. My words are not pure native words, they're pure *spirit* words. My heritage is of the spirit. . .as everyone's is. I am not a native writer. I am a writer of *spirituality*. That's why I came. That's the only reason I'm alive.

Within the pile of correspondence I came across another letter that was steeped in hate. This woman was calling herself the true leader of the Spirit Clan. The letter came from Minnesota. She used obscene language in bold writing. She said I was to stop receiving gifts from my friends at the Valhalla shop in Manitou Springs. She said I was to stay off Indian lands. She claimed to be the living head of the Anasazi tribe. Also within her acerbic language was a clear threat. She called upon her USAF friends and those of the reserve and enlistment centers all over the country who (she claimed) she had connections with. These others were watching me all the time and she hoped I'd sleep well tonight.

Dear God, this native woman went into my Prayer Smoke that night. Her letter also went to the sheriff's office for their Summer Rain "threat" file.

What disgusted me was not the threat this woman inferred, but how she could claim *head* of anything *spiritual* and, at the same time, use such obscene words and make life threats. These things just are not possible for a highly evolved soul. Another aspect of her claims that amused me to no end was the fact that she claimed *leadership* of the Anasazi *Spirit Clan*. Know what? I *protected* the sacredness of that clan's title. I used a pseudonym for it when I began writing of the Anasazi. Now

I see proof of that wisdom. I cannot count the number of people who have claimed Spirit Clan connections. I cannot count the numbers who are fooling themselves. I cannot count the number of times I was thankful I'd protected the Clan's sacredness. Whoever this native woman thinks she is, she is not connected to the Anasazi in any way, shape or form. How sad. How sad it is to have the need to be someone you're not. How sad it is to be so uncomfortable with the who of who you came to be.

Love.

Hate.

I have many friends who work up in Cripple Creek at the casinos there. The employees are good mountain folk working at the best opportunities for income in the region.

At one casino, where several of my friends and readers are employed, there is a young native man by the name of Marty. A few times when I've been in there, he sat and talked with me, but recently, he had a special package to present to me. His cousin, Jerry Lessert, is a Sioux medicine man and he had blessed a large bundle of sacred sage for me. I was moved beyond words when I received the beautiful gift. It felt so full of life when I took it into my hands. Even as a writer, I'm at a loss of words to properly express how full my heart was to know that a Sioux medicine man had made and blessed this sage for me.

Love.

And so, for me, this last expression of warm sentiment holds strong within my heart. It fills it up. This one gesture came to be all I'll ever need to settle the native issue within me. Others can still hate. Others can still pen their little obscene words, but for me, I am now at peace with the issue. I have my blessed bundle of sage. Its simple sacredness has triumphed over hate. That is what it symbolizes for me. . .peace.

As a return gift to the medicine man, I sent Jerry signed copies of *Ancient Echoes* and *Whispered Wisdom* with a note expressing my gratitude for his kindness. Just recently I heard that he's now planning on using *Ancient Echoes* in their children's school as a prayer and chant book.

Love.

# FORCING TIME

At the beginning of February, Robin came to us with an idea she'd been tossing around in her mind for the last few months. She wanted our thoughts on it. She'd been thinking of moving out. Her reasons were varied; however, we all knew the family's home life hadn't been a bed of roses for the last few months. Personally, I thought her idea was a good one because she and Mandy shouldn't have to be constantly exposed to the problems that'd been plaguing our family relationships. Also, being connected to people who kept getting death threats was more than a little unnerving too. Who wants to be inadvertently caught in some possible cross-fire? Who'd want to be mistaken for me on some dark night?

Bill and I agreed that her idea was not going to hurt our feelings and that she'd most likely enjoy being alone with

Mandy in their own little place in Woodland Park. The idea was placed on the back burner for a while. Meanwhile, Bill and I had some serious issues to consider.

If Robin moved out we'd be down a third of our house payment source. We worked and reworked budget figures. Our income taxes took a chunk of our own income and that portion was not free to be spendable on a larger part of a house payment. When all was gone over and over again, we saw we were in trouble. We'd purchased the house for the seven of us. Three incomes were required to keep it.

On Friday, February 19th, we had our real estate friend, Jane Stiffler, over for the evening. We needed to sell the house. We discussed what we had decided to look for—a small place—a real small place that we could comfortably afford. So we put the Wildhorn house on the market and began to search for something we could all live with.

Because our friend had bought the house next to us as his getaway place, I thought it only fair to call him and let him know what we were forced to do. I didn't think it'd do our friendship much good to have him find out through another source.

Bill disagreed with me. We disagreed a lot lately. He didn't want our friend to know we'd put the house on the market. Bill strongly felt that he wouldn't understand why we had to do it. But I insisted.

Bill called our friend.

I watched the one-sided conversation take place. I watched Bill's face redden and heard his voice become irritated. I listened as he explained over and over again why we had to sell. Finally the conversation was over.

"Guess what?" he said. "Remember the down payment money Jim gifted us with? He wants it back now."

I was shocked. "You're kidding."

Bill shook his head. "Do I look like I'm kidding? Jim said that the money was a gift for getting our dream home. If this isn't our dream home after all, he wants his money back."

"But we don't have it!"

"I told him that. He said he'd wait until we sold the house and take it out of what we make. He was really mad that we might make a profit."

"But look at all the improvements we've done. There was no horse stall or corral here when we moved in. There was no wallpaper or paneling or Z-Brick on the walls then. We've done a ton to this place since moving in. How can he begrudge a little profit? Besides, we have to make something on it in order to buy something else."

Bill's head was shaking. "Go figure. Jim says he didn't give us the money to *make* money with."

"But we never *planned* on ever selling this place."

He looked about the room. "Yeah, this was the dream house, wasn't it."

I sighed. "More like a nightmare house, if you ask me."

He was silent.

"So what do we do?" I asked.

"Do? Nothing. We do nothing."

A few days later we received a letter from Jim's brother, who did all his dirtier work. In the letter, he proposed that we pay back the money out of profits from the house sale and that Jane, our realtor, could keep it in escrow for Jim. Willie said that his brother would never give someone money for the purpose of *making* money.

We took the letter to our attorney and discussed the entire situation with him. His only question was: "Was anything signed? Such as an I.O.U. or promissory note?" The answer was a definitive "No." In fact, at the time Jim offered us help toward our downpayment, his words were, "Let me help you with the down payment. I have a little karma to clear." His gift was a gift.

Our attorney suggested we do nothing about Willie's letter of demand. He said we were under no legal obligation to repay someone's freely-given gift.

We returned home and put Jim's house key into an envelope and mailed it back to him. We'd had it over a period of months so we could keep an eye on his place when he wasn't around. We'd check it for signs of break-in, make sure his heat was up enough to prevent broken water pipes, etc. Sending the key back was our final word on the subject. We never heard from Jim (or Willie) again.

What disturbs me about this whole thing is the fact that I'd

Mountain view from the porch of Grand Central Station

(Left to right)
Sarah, Aimee,
and Jenny

Photographing the
Marble Valley for pictorial

Aimee during the fire
department's practice day
(Photo by Kyle)

At Virginia
Beach after
the deposition

Sarah's first time
in an ocean

Jenny having fun
feeding the sea gulls

The Changeling House
on Wildhorn Road

Readers' gifts grace my native room in the Wildhorn house

Me and Tee

Loving Valor

Playing with Valor

Valor playing back

The ghostly Pale Rider

Sarah, Aimee,
Mandy,
and Robin

Sarah and Magic
having one of
their special
"moments"

My new baby,
Cheyenne

Bill intently
watching my
Greystone
interview

Greystone interview for NBC's TV special, *Ancient Prophecies*

Ghost Trail Marker
relocated to cabin

Farmer Brown (Bill)
playing on the backhoe

Our little corner of paradise

Sarah's graduation
photo (by Proex)

Aimee and
Robert's
wedding
reception

Bill grading our
mountain road

Sarah and Jeff

Jenny and Bill

Aimee and Robert

Cheyenne, grown
and ever watchful

Big Horn sheep
in our drive

Pinecone (rt) and her mama, "Baby"

Pinecone kissing Cheyenne

Woodswalking at my cabin

Laughing with Snow Maker

A bittersweet winter

saved Jim from spending over twenty thousand do
couple of frequency healing machines he was int
getting hold of. He'd call Bill and ask if Mary could p
check out the machines to see if they were accurate
done this twice. And we'd even kept one of the better
hidden at our own house during times when he felt
able having it at his own. . .we'd protected his
behind a time or two. The government agencies w
the trail of the maker of these machines and Will
words with these agents when they came to raid th
residence. Willie had gotten out by the skin of his
time.

Bill and I had no interest in these frequency ma
there sure were a heck of a lot of folks who we
abounded around our house for quite a while. We
hands on a fairly accurate machine, except for
frequencies that were "off" and we wouldn't use th
some good things with it. I was even preparing to
Bear in an attempt to help him when I heard that
late. One's destiny doesn't wait. Instead, I sent
into my Prayer Smoke.

So it seemed that our connection with Jim and
been completely severed. Jim still visited his mo
once in a while, but he never called or stopped
bumped into one of our girls and had heard that B
been having problems, yet he never approached

In February we had two showings for the house
complained that it wasn't remote enough becaus
still hear airplanes. I think those folks want an
Where can you live without hearing planes?

The second couple was far more promising, y
about them made me uneasy. The man was
semi-famous horse trainer who was looking fo
train and stable horses. He loved the place and
land. He gave indication that he was very intere
we'd hear back because he'd need to walk the
before an offer would be forthcoming. We were
deal would be cash. He'd had some investors t
participate in his planned operation.

And so we thought we might have a buyer. If this panned out, we'd need to locate another place fairly quickly and put an offer on it before someone else did. Properties in the Woodland Park and Pikes Peak region were going fast. People were moving into the area like bees on honey. Prices were climbing higher and higher by the week. Rentals were scarce and, what there were of them, were skyrocketing. Now that we needed a small place—nothing much was available to choose from. When something was found, we needed to jump on it right away before another offer beat us to it. Our friends began to tease me about all my readers moving here and leaving no place for me to go. Oh well, whatever was available we'd pick from those. It probably wouldn't be what we'd envisioned, but at least we'd have a roof over our heads. And isn't that all that really matters anyway? What we didn't know at the time was that we'd tried to force time by putting our house on the market. What we didn't know then was that our prospective buyer was not who he seemed. What we didn't know then was that someone was out to financially ruin us. How could that be? Well, that's an entirely different story to tell, but there was an individual in our lives who had stated that he'd do that if he ever could. I guess he had friends.

# AND THEN THERE WERE FIVE

For the rest of February, Robin went in search of a place for her and Mandy. Rob decided that living out in Florissant was too inconvenient and thought that residing right in Woodland Park would be easier for her and Mandy to accommodate their individual activities. Mandy could walk to school. Robin would be within a couple minutes from work at City Market.

At this time, Robin was also entertaining the idea of going to massage school. She was very interested in the natural healing field and doing some sort of energy work. This would entail her traveling down Ute Pass to the Colorado Springs massage school many times a week.

The rental houses that were available were not suitable to her for various reasons. Money was a factor, of course. Handling the entire rent herself was an aspect that greatly limited her options. Eventually she told us of two places that appeared to be good possibilities. We discussed the pros and cons of each and she decided on a little blue house set among tall pines. I thought it was cute as a bug and just right for the two of them. It had two bedrooms which was something they'd done without for quite a long while. There was a stone fireplace and also a propane Warm Morning heater in the living room. The place had a quaint atmosphere to it and I knew they'd love it.

On March 3rd, Robin and Mandy moved out of our Wildhorn house. Friends from her work helped with the move because we couldn't. We had several houses scheduled to look at that day and our appointments began bright and early.

Jane took us to a wonderful log place out by Westcreek. I'd always admired the house from afar, and now it was for sale. I fell in love with it. Bill was a little less enthusiastic because of man-type concerns like a shallow spring for water, visibility from Highway 67, the need for a new roof, etc. Granted, these needed consideration given to them, but I didn't see them being anything major. As far as the house being highly visible from the highway, well, who's going to stop on a narrow curve and pull out binoculars or a rifle?

What enhanced this property even more was the fact that it also had a little two-bedroom log cabin on it that was rented. Perfect for one or two of our girls. They were getting to the point where they could certainly stand living separate from us. I liked the idea of them living in their own little place, yet close by. I loved the property.

The next place Jane took us to was located off Teller 1 in the mountain community called Highland Meadows. You got to it by driving up a twisting mountain road and then down and around into a small valley. The house itself was nothing much to look at from the outside but the inside was laid out perfectly. It even had a solarium area beside the kitchen. It was sitting on three fenced acres where deer came to graze. The owner commented that she'd tried and tried to grow shrubs and flowers, but the deer would graze right up to the porch and eat all her lilac and rose bushes down to stubs. She showed us pictures of them to prove it. I liked the house a lot because the three bedrooms were well-placed and the view was wonderful. Bill, on the other hand, was quickly slipping out of the house-hunting mood. He'd become irritated at something and began pointing out how questionable that mountain road would be in the winter to negotiate if it became icy. He wanted to leave. He wasn't all that interested in this place. We left.

For the next few days we hadn't heard anything more from Jane because there were no more properties in our price range to look at. Bill was irritable and frequently fell into melancholy. He'd go to bed early to get away from the family. During the day, we'd find ways to avoid him too. Things were not peaceful. And I hated it.

The following week we went out again but nothing seemed to feel right for us. Time became a pressure issue that pressed us forward. We had an offer on our Wildhorn house and needed to find a place to move to before the closing date. So far only the two properties were options and Bill didn't care for either one. We couldn't look at anything more expensive nor could we consider smaller places because we still had the three girls to accommodate. This made our range of options very narrow, and there just wasn't a lot to pick from. It seemed we were down to the two. It was a discouraging situation because Bill wasn't drawn to either one and I needed him to at least like whatever we bought.

When Jane again called us, we thought she'd found us another property to see. This was not her reason for contacting us. It seemed that our buyer was requesting an extension on our contract. He was still gathering his investors and it looked as though it would take a little longer than initially thought. We granted the extension for him. The extension gave us more time to find something Bill would be more interested in.

We had a breather.

# WEE HEART CALLING

Life in the Wildhorn house altered after Robin and Mandy left. They'd been living with us for so long that it felt like part of our family was missing. Indeed, they were part of our family by now and I did miss their presence. With Bill going through his difficult time and Aimee working down at the hospital and Sarah in school, I was alone much of the time, for Bill was out for most of the day.

Taking solace in the woods became my only comfort during this time. I had no close friend—I never had anyone to really talk personal things over with, nor had I anyone who would just sit and put their arms around me while I cried. No one to hold me. Now when I went into the woods my former companions were nowhere to be found. They too had left me alone during this trying time Bill and I were going through. So nature itself gave its heart to me. I received it with open arms and, in return, gifted back my falling tears that only Grandmother Earth felt fall upon her breast.

This is how life was. This was how I walked through my days of being so alone. Yet there were diamonds among those days too. One such day came on Sunday, March 14th, when I'd finally gotten tired of having nothing to read. I asked Bill if he wanted to take a run downtown to the Citadel Mall because I needed to go to the bookstore. He wasn't thrilled with the idea; however, he saw that going somewhere together might make the day a little less depressing for us.

Bill was never one for browsing through shops so he stayed out in the van while I went in search of a few gold nuggets in Waldenbooks. It seemed that, more and more, I had a difficult time finding books that interest me. I'm not attracted to fiction, metaphysical works usually end up being boring, and Native American issues become redundant after reading the first few, since facts are facts and you can only arrange the words in a limited number of ways. Historical biographies interest me sometimes, depending on who the book is about. I like reading Irving Stone and Michener. Philosophy had long ago lost its appeal to me because, in essence, spiritual reality far surpasses such humanistic thought. Certain physics books spark my attention, like the time I picked up a couple great ones that included *The Holographic Universe*. That one made me smile as I read it because it hit on some extremely critical facts that my Starman had revealed to me about reality and how all of life is related through the vibrational frequency of one strand of DNA that is God's own essence. Oh yes, I found a few points in this book that the author didn't get just right, but on the whole, he had the germ of the right idea. I was impressed.

So now I found myself once again perusing the thousands of books, looking for just one or two that would prove worth my while. It wasn't an easy task and often proved more frustrating than fun. Eventually I found one and as I searched for another, something kept pulling my attention away from the stacks of books. I looked out to the mall area. Nobody was looking at me. The sensation that someone was silently addressing me from that direction was strong. When I didn't spot the source I returned to the bookshelves and tried to give them my full attention. No good. Again I felt the pull. I turned again. People were passing by the doorway yet nobody was just standing there looking in. I glanced at those around me in the shop. They were inert. My feelings were not coming from any of these people.

My heart lunged then. Why it did so I couldn't say. When that happened there was usually an important reason. I went to the front of the shop and stood in the doorway, looking right and left. I just stood there acting like a radar screen trying to zone in on where this magnetic pull was coming from. The left. It was stronger to my left.

I turned my back on the force and went to the counter to pay for the three books I'd found. Then, quickly, I walked out to the left.

Beep-Beep-Beep. My radar was getting louder.

Pound-Pound-Pound. My heart was beating harder.

My internal sensors had brought me to the door of a pet shop.

Was someone in there that I'm meant to meet today? This was naturally my first thought because that's how things work with me.

I entered and stood just inside the doorway. I scanned the people milling about. No one drew my attention, yet the beeping became stronger and heart pounded like a pile-driver. Someone was in here that I had to meet.

I turned slightly to face an altered direction. The beeping lessened. I turned back and followed the strongest signals. I walked through the shop, listening and feeling. I was thrown off when the strongest signals came when I wasn't facing a person. This made me frown. What was going on here? Yet as I neared the space devoid of people, the signals began to quicken and boom.

Beep-beep-beep-beep. BEEP-BEEP-BEEP-BEEP!

Boom-boom-boom-boom. BOOM-BOOM-BOOM-BOOM! Went my heart.

I was standing in front of a cage.

A tiny grey ball of fluff with a black nose and mouth was frantically trying to get my attention.

BEEP-BEEP-BEEP!
BOOM-BOOM-BOOM!
Oh, *GOD!*

My hand hit my chest. If I didn't know better I would've sworn my heart actually did a somersault.

Jumping up and down on stubby little legs and whimpering for all she was worth, the tiny pup didn't take her big blue eyes off me.

Nor could I take mine from hers.

Finally, I raced to the counter. "Excuse me," I rudely interrupted the clerk, "what kind of dog is that grey one with the black face?"

"That's a Keeshond, miss."

"Thank you," I muttered, rushing back to the heartbeat.

"Keeshond?" I whispered to myself. I'd never heard of the breed.

The furry grey ball had been watching me go and return. It jumped up off its tiny legs now. "Take me! *Take* me! I'm supposed to be with you! Hold me! *Hold* me!"

I jumped when the clerk touched my shoulder. "Do you want me to get her out for you? Do you want to see her?"

My thoughts were a jumble. Never. *Never* was I going to get another puppy. *Never* was I going to give it my heart and then have it broken when it died.

I must've looked like a zombie when my eyes met those of the kind clerk.

"I don't. . .I. . .I don't. . .I'll be right back!" And I fled the shop.

Out in the parking lot I banged on Bill's window. "Will you come in the mall with me? I wanna show you something."

He gave me one of those looks. You know the kind—disgusted or the "what now?" look. But he came just the same.

"You went into the pet shop, didn't you," he said with a knowing grin.

My face lit up. I didn't have to answer. I was pulling him through the parking lot—literally pulling him.

When he stood before the cage, he smiled wide. "What is it? It looks like a bear cub with a muddy face."

The clerk returned. "Do you want to see her now?" she asked.

Before I could open my mouth, Bill said we would. And we were led into a tiny cubby room where customers could "visit" with their prospective purchases.

Oh. Oh! Holding that wee bit of squirming fluff filled my heart up and made it overflow all over her. She snuggled around my neck and did all she could to wriggle her way further into my heart. Tears came to my eyes.

I held her out to Bill. "You hold her and see what you think."

She was a handful. "She's awful squirmy," he said handing her back. "I think she's partial to you. You want to get her?"

I held the tiny bear-like cub up to my chin and nuzzled her face. "Oh Bill, I don't know. It hurts so much to lose them."

We were silent for a few minutes while I snuggled the warm ball with the muddy face.

A man and woman strolled past the visiting room door. "Oh," exclaimed the man, "you got a little Keeshond there! We bought one a few months ago and we never regretted it. Our baby is the best little companion you'd ever find. You're gonna love having her around." And they passed on.

Companion? Someone to hold and love me back?

I lifted the bit of fluff up to my eyes and looked hard into the big blues that stared back.

I whispered a wordless question to her. "What do you think, Little Mudface, shall we go home together?"

She didn't move, not even a wriggle. She only stared back and, beneath my thumb, I felt the tiny heart drumming out a fast and furious new cadence.

We had silently communicated.

I shifted my eyes over to Bill. "I'd like to take her home with us."

He smiled. "I knew that as soon as I saw her. C'mon, let's go see about getting her outta here."

On the long drive back to Florissant, Little Mudface slept in Bill's lap. He liked that. I knew how much he was enjoying the little one so I didn't make any move to hold her. I'd have plenty of time for that. After all, I was always the one to housetrain these new pups. She and I would be inseparable for many months to come. We wouldn't need bonding. . .we already had. My heart was soothed that someone had been sent to love me back. I wouldn't be alone anymore. I had a companion. . .one who spoke my wordless language of love.

After a few weeks of being with the pup constantly, I named her Cheyenne. That was inherently her name. Yet as I watched her hilarious antics of charging here and there in a nonstop fashion, I began calling her Chu-Chu for the runaway locomotive she resembled during these wildly active spurts of energy. Then when she began chewing on everything in sight, Chu-Chu was even more fitting. My little Chu-Chu. My little love.

Our vet had offered to give us free animal care in return for Bill's gift of Valor to him. When Joel came out to give Chu-Chu her shots, he gave us a little background on the Keeshond breed. He said to be sure to get her used to strangers before she got too much older. This caution was because Keeshonds are the dog breed closest to the wolf in respect to how they view their "pack." Those outside the pack are looked on as enemies. Joel said that Chu-Chu could select certain family members and make them her own pack members—everyone else would be enemy in her mind. That surprised me. Chu and I were already close. Of course I loved that, but also didn't want her to be threatening to others who came around.

Eventually Chu accepted everyone in the family and, once she got to know friends, they too were accepted in her pack. With strangers she's guarded and watchful. She's the best guard dog we've ever had. She's my companion. She's so much my companion that, when I go out into my Prayer Place in the woods and my consciousness slips deeply into altered states while praying, she maintains a twenty-yard perimeter around my circle and then occasionally will come into it to double-check on me. There are times when I've fallen asleep upon Grandmother's breast following my communion with her and Chu will make sure I'm not out in the snowy winter night too long. Her gentle kisses awaken me. She loves the woods as much as I do. She's my little woodswalking companion. . .always.

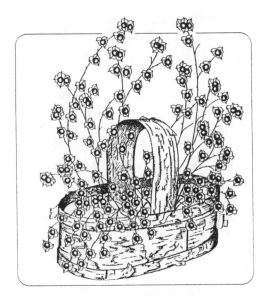

# AND THEN THERE WERE THREE

While Aimee was employed by a Colorado Springs hospital, her twenty-first birthday rolled around. As a family, we wanted to do something extra special to mark this occasion in a unique way. This was accomplished by taking the family and a few of our close friends into Cripple Creek to spend the evening. This date had been the first time we'd been there since the dozens of craft shops had been converted over to casinos. Between meeting up with other friends who were employed at the various establishments, Aimee and Jenny were carded time and time again. Although Jenny was twenty-three at the time, she looked fourteen, and Aimee didn't look a day over sixteen. Sarah, being underage, was never carded because she stayed well away from the front of the gaming machines.

Initially, on a personal level, I was somewhat intimidated

by the glitzy decor and my own ignorance of how the slot machines worked. Our friend, Frank Gonzalez, worked at the Phenix House Casino at the time and he explained how they operated and the difference between the kinds of slots. I felt like a real mountain hick.

We found it interesting to mosey in and out of the many casinos, for their decor varied as much as their amusing names. The Midnight Rose, Bronco Billy's, The Gold Rush, Creeker's, The Aspen Mine. Each unique, yet most a variation on the Old West or Gold Mining Town theme.

The few shops that remained in business were also crowded the evening we visited Cripple Creek. The one I particularly like to browse through is Cripple Creek Treasures because of the wonderful locally-mined turquoise the owner and her partner extract from Grandmother Earth. Grandmother certainly has an unlimited wealth of beauty that She gifts us with! The other shop I always find something interesting in is The Little Lode. This place is packed with unique items that are far removed from the expected tourist-type of stock. This is where I picked up a little Yield sign that said KEESHOND CROSSING. Of course this was specifically for Chu-Chu. Another shop was a general store that had been in operation in Cripple Creek for many, many years. It was famous for its old-time atmosphere and ice cream cones. The other shops were mostly jewelry stores that carried gold and Native American items.

We browsed a few of these shops, but were mostly in town for a fun evening of discovering the casinos. Aimee had a lot of fun and we wrapped up the night by treating everyone to dinner at Maggie's Place. This restaurant was one of the quieter eateries in town because it was located below street level far away from the noise of the Colorado Grande Casino above it.

With full stomachs and pockets empty of our coins, we left Cripple Creek satisfied that we'd managed to mark Aimee's day as being the special one we'd hoped it'd be. That March 24th would be remembered for a long time to come.

By the time April came, Aimee had become discontented with the amount of politics that invaded her hospital job. More than a few times she'd been reprimanded for spending so much time at a patient's bedside. She worked on the cardiac floor and would return home with heartbreaking tales of how this elderly patient or that one never had any visitors. She always tried to take a personal interest in these by sitting beside their beds and giving them extra attention and conversation. This compassion had a down side that reared its painful head when she'd go in to work and learn that one of her patients had died during the night. A few of these hit her hard. Although she accepted these deaths, what she found most difficult to deal with was the lack of time she was allotted for one-on-one touching type of visiting with the more lonely patients. This, more than anything, she could not deal with. So eventually she gave her notice and was back home during the day again.

Since Aimee needed to look for work, she thought she'd take a break from the medical field. The only decent paying game in the area was the casinos in Cripple Creek. Many of our mountain friends had already secured jobs there and Aimee figured she'd give it a go too; after all, from where we lived, the town was a straight shot up Teller 1.

At this same time, Jenny was getting antsy being at home all the time. She would make comments about having no friends or never getting out to meet anyone who might turn out to become a boyfriend. She'd mention now and then about getting married and having kids. This was clear indication that she was ready to try working out in the world again. This was something I was waiting for. She needed to get out. She needed friends. I hated seeing her stuck in the house day after day, but she'd always shied away from the idea of working every time I brought it up. . .until now.

Our friend Linda Gonzalez worked at The Gold Rush casino and understood Jenny's learning disability. Linda offered to hire Jenny as a porter and give her special attention in training and personal guidance. Jenny seemed to like the idea. Therefore, both Jenny and Aimee got jobs at The Gold Rush. Aimee started out as a porter like Jenny, then switched to cocktail waitressing. A casino was not either of their first choices for employment, but when that's the best paying option around for fifty miles, you don't shun the opportunity.

Since the girls' shifts sometimes varied and Jenny didn't

drive, a transportation problem developed. The best solution for this was for Jenny and Aimee to rent a small house in Cripple Creek so Jenny could walk back and forth to work. This was discussed in great detail and everyone agreed that that was the best way to go. We found them a tiny one-bedroom Victorian two blocks from their casino. They moved in and began their first step at independence. We were proud of how they split their bills and managed so well on their own. Bill had to replace their living room heater with an extra propane Warm Morning one we'd had for many years. When he got into revamping the vent pipe, he found that the chimney was completely blocked with crumbled cement and bricks. He had Aimee take photos of the dangerous condition and read the riot act to their landlord for having a life-threatening situation in one of his rentals. The girls could've died from carbon monoxide poisoning in their sleep. Bill was furious, for he'd seen enough people getting sick from just such a situation. He cleaned out the flue and angled the vent properly for good draw. We filed away the photos for future use.

Eventually, Jenny did find her boyfriend. David was a forty-year-old gentleman who worked security. He was drawn to Jenny's gentle nature. They began going out to dinner after work. They had common spiritual beliefs. They loved being together and often passed notes to one another during work hours. In time, Jenny spent more and more time down at his apartment in Cañon City—this being a situation I adamantly disagreed with, but accepted. Jenny was nearly twenty-four and, although she tended to cling to new friends, she needed to make her own choices in life. The situation was one we never agreed on and whenever I'd try to advise her to spend more time at her Cripple Creek house, she'd give me the old statement that she was on her own now and I couldn't tell her what to do. Well, she was right about that, but didn't a parent still have the right to an experienced opinion? I stopped bringing it up whenever I talked with her on the phone. We got along much better that way.

Aimee too found a new gentleman friend who worked at the casino. He was in his thirties, divorced, and had two beautiful little boys who lived with him. Robert was the bartender who invited Aimee out to dinner. Initially she confided to me that she was in no way interested in dating for a while. She'd just come off of an unpleasant relationship with a co-worker at the hospital and didn't want to jump right into another. She wanted some space. Yet, I heard her words and her actions didn't justify with them. She told me about more and more dinner dates with Robert. She raved about his beautiful blond little boys. Uh-huh. Yep. The signs were all there. Right Aimee.

So both girls had new boyfriends. Both enjoyed working and being independent. Both were happy.

We, on the other hand, were down to just our income for the big Wildhorn house. We were tightening our belts as tight as they'd go. The situation was reaching critical mass. Our May 17th closing date had been postponed. Another delay came and went. Our buyer requested additional time to get his investors in a row. Being the trusting souls we were, we agreed. We agreed because we trusted this individual even though I had twinges of something I couldn't put my finger on. Suspicion. Something not quite right with the deal or the buyer. Yet I pushed them aside in order to let hope and trust remain in the forefront. What ate up a large portion of our income was our self-employment taxes. We had to automatically set aside a certain percentage of each royalty check to save for the quarterly estimated income taxes we sent in. This cut down our useable money considerably. So we sucked in our stomachs and tightened our belts one more notch in order to not lose the house before it sold.

With our house down to just three dwellers, I found myself alone a lot. Sarah was active with her new boyfriend, Jeff, all the time. He had horses they rode often and the two had so much in common that it was eerie. They loved rappelling off boulders, hiking, mountain biking, horse riding, and skiing in the winter. Jeff was on the Ski Patrol at Ski Cooper in Leadville. He taught Sarah how to ski and, the very first time he took her out he had her going down the Black Runs. These, I heard, were the hardest runs reserved for the more experienced skiers. Jeff said he'd been impressed with Sarah's performance on these. Good thing I knew nothing about it until after the fact. Those two little daredevils try things that'd make a mother's heart stop! Yet, when I think about it I say "why not?" That's not her dad's perspective though. So we've learned to keep a few little adventures from him. It's a far, far better thing that we do this.

With Sarah being gone much of the time and Bill being gone to Cassie's office or her home to help with his counselling, I was alone most days. We'd given the old pickup to Aimee to use and Bill had the van. I was left with a couple bikes in the garage. Or I could drive the old Farm All tractor Frank Gonzalez had left parked at the house for Bill to use on the long drive. Other than those means of transportation I was housebound on a daily basis and it was driving me nuts. I'm not one to leave the mountains much, but gosh, there are times when I'd like to go somewhere even if it's just for a mountain drive.

Then, when I received a letter from Pocket that contained my royalty statement for *Earthway*, I was pleased to see how well the volume was selling. This check, after we set aside a piece of the pie for Uncle Sam, would tide us over for a while and give me something to put down on a vehicle for me to use. And I knew just the inexpensive little one I wanted. . .another little red Storm.

When I got up a few mornings later, I went downstairs and approached Bill.

"Sarah's going with me to buy a car today. Want to come along?"

The look on his face could've stopped a train. He couldn't speak.

"Did you hear me? I'm buying a car today. Want to come or not?"

"A car?"

"Yes. A car. I'm tired of being stuck in the house every day with no way to go anywhere. I need transportation too."

"But I always take you everywhere you need to go."

I smiled. "You're never home anymore. You're always at Cassie's." I picked up my purse. "You coming?"

That evening a little red Storm followed the van up the mountain pass to our house. That evening a tiny car was parked in the bay next to the one housing Bill's van. That evening I felt as though I'd sprouted wings. It was June 3rd.

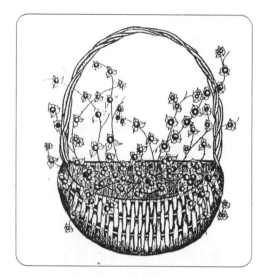

# PARADISE FOUND

Our purchase contract for the Wildhorn house was still active, although the longer we extended it, the less sure we were of it being a valid offer. I kept thinking of the man who said he could financially ruin us. I wondered if our buyers were his friends keeping us on a long tether. Regardless, the offer was on the table and that meant we needed to find another dwelling to move into if and when the deal finally did close.

On June 6th, our real estate friend, Jane Stiffler, drove us out to a small cabin on thirty acres within a rural residential area called Four Mile Ranches.

Bumpy dirt roads led us around curving lanes through open spaces interspersed with tall stands of fir and pine. Jane turned right and, after passing over a cattle guard, drove up another curving road that was actually the cabin's drive. We pulled up beside a small place set among towering evergreens.

The dwelling had two tiny bedrooms; one barely large enough for a twin bed, the other squeezing in a queen. Kitchen area was what is often referred to as a galley type and there was a small bathroom. But it was the living room that pulled at me. It was long and wide. The owner had built it onto the original cabin and had done a beautiful job. Pine paneling on all four walls and ceiling, but overlaying the ceiling wood were enormous logs extending the width of the room. A huge fireplace was set in at one end of the room, while at the other end, large windows and sliding glass doors gave exit to a rustic covered porch area. The whole place was not more than 1,100 sq. ft., but it had the definite feel of home.

Outside, behind the house, was a log root cellar built into a hillock covered with pine. Off to the left was a pond that the owner kept filled by way of piping from a natural spring at the back of the acreage. Deer, bear, and other critters drank from this natural pool. Their prints could be seen in the surrounding muddy banks.

Wildlife abounded around this property. Coyotes howled and packs hunched on the various rises. A great horned owl nested high in the pines. A bear roamed alongside the house in the evening and emptied the birdfeeders by night. Mountain squirrels were tame enough to come into the owner's house for the bread he hand-fed them. Little sure-footed chipmunks scampered about while a multitude of birds chirped in the fir boughs. Bunnies had warrens beneath the house. Hawks flew overhead. A family of foxes burrowed nearby. What more could I ask for? We'd found our Paradise.

We talked to the owner, who wintered in Florida. He was getting tired of carting belongings back and forth each year and wanted to unload the cabin. We came to a verbal agreement regarding purchase price and he was willing to wait to do a formal contract until we were certain of our own buyer. Meanwhile, we'd decided it may not be a bad idea to mention the fact that our Wildhorn house was on the market in the Hampton Roads newsletter. We were sure that at least one of the many people planning on relocating to Colorado would be interested in our house if the present offer fell through. We tried to cover our backsides this way.

We drove away from the tiny cabin full of excitement. We'd finally found our little piece of Paradise and, although we had to put it on hold for the moment, looked forward to the day we'd actually be moving in.

A week later, while Bill and I were working down in our office area, he surprised me.

"I want to get you special plates for your Storm. Think of something different."

"How many letters do I get?" I grinned.

"Seven."

"I want it to read NO-EYES!"

He rolled his eyes. "Right. You put that on your license plate and everyone will know who's driving. Everyone will know where you live too."

That scenario never entered my mind. I frowned. "How about STARMAN then. That'd be okay, wouldn't it?"

Now he frowned. "Maybe not. You talked about your starman in *Soul Sounds*. People might still make the connection." Then his eyes lit up. "I know, how about U.F.O.!"

My expression matched his. And a few weeks later, the little red UFO was streaking up and down Highway 24. What a tickle I got out of piloting my unidentified flying object through the mountains. What a kick people's comments gave me.

# FACING DOWN THE BIG EYE

On Monday, July 12th, I was hit with the one request I'd been dreading for years. Bob Friedman at Hampton Roads called Bill to discuss the best way to approach me on the subject of me doing an interview for a major television production on prophecies. Both Bob and Bill were well aware of my deep-seated need for privacy and how adamantly I shunned cameras and reporters. To say I shunned them may be the wrong way to put it. I just didn't like being before the public eye in any way, and print interviews, especially newspaper ones, never failed to misquote me or slant the articles in some negative manner. After this was proven out a couple of times, I was no longer interested in attempting to put forth the truth and have it colored by a reporter's personal attitude or perspective. All cameras are a taboo issue with me. I don't like having my picture taken because I'm basically shy. I'm just too committed to keeping myself out of the public eye and prefer the background position that a messenger should strive to maintain.

So Bob and Bill talked about approaching me with this new development. Bill got off the phone and came over to me.

"I just got off the phone with Bob. Sit down, we need to discuss something after I run it by you."

I rolled my eyes. "If you just got through talking to Bob, you two are in cahoots over some publicity thing again. I told you I'm not doing anything."

He sat beside me. "You do booksignings."

"That's not fair. You know why I do those. Getting out and touching my readers in a personal way is important to me. That's not the same at all."

Bill seemed determined this time. He appeared to prepare a convincing argument on Bob's behalf.

"Just listen for a minute. This is something really different. It's not just some little interview or TV talk show."

I raised a brow. "Just how different are we talking here?"

He hesitated. "A major NBC-TV special on prophecies. The tentative title is *Ancient Prophecies*."

A big NBC-TV special? I didn't think so. No, I was sure I didn't think so.

"No way, Bill. There's no way I'm going before a camera on national television. Nope." And I shook my head to prove it.

He sighed. "Listen. It's going to be a two-hour special and they're doing Edgar Cayce, Nostradamus, and people like that. NBC contracted Greystone Communications, Inc. to produce the program and the people at Greystone kept hearing your name pop up while doing their initial research. They want to include you in the program."

"That's nice but I don't *do* cameras."

His shoulders dropped.

Mine raised. "What's the matter with Bob anyway? He knows how strongly I feel about publicity. How could he give even a ray of hope for something this big? As far as any publicity goes, I've told him to just view me as a deceased author. How can this Greystone interview a dead author?"

His eyes hardened.

Mine softened. I smiled. "Well?"

Bill was growing exasperated with my stubbornness. He hated it when I wouldn't even give a few minutes of serious consideration to a new proposal. I had the habit of rejecting them out of hand no matter what they involved or how important the exposure could be for my material.

"Mary," he sighed, "you're not thinking this through. Millions of people will be watching that special. Millions."

I laughed at that thought. "Yeah, that's exactly why I don't want to be before that camera. I can't even imagine me being seen by so many. It just doesn't suit me. I'm not the kind of person that should be out there with the others they're thinking of using."

Now his voice became a little stronger. "You belong there as much as they do. No-Eyes' prophecies are timely and accurate. They're relevant and current. What better way to fit her message in than a major TV special on the subject?" He frowned. "The information you have in *Phoenix Rising* and all the maps you included in *Daybreak* are just what these people are looking for. Don't you see how many more people you could reach by doing this?"

He was playing on my strong sense of purpose, yet I wouldn't allow it to affect me. "The books have been doing just fine through word of mouth. I don't have to do big publicity things to get the word out. They stand alone. They're already out and running all on their own, thank you very much."

Bill again sighed. He stood and turned to walk away. "I'm not calling Bob back until you've thought more on this. You need to understand what you're turning down here."

I watched him go. I watched him go and knew there was no way I was going to change my mind. Imagine! Me on national TV! No way.

As the day wore on the issue of this exposure wouldn't leave my mind. I thought and thought on it, all the while absolutely certain I would not do it.

In the late evening, after I'd finished going through a large stack of readership mail and I'd had some free time at my desk, I sat back and began rubbing my stomach. It was doing that odd kind of quivering that only comes from the solar plexus region when something is trying to get my serious attention. That attention could only be the TV special.

Suddenly my thoughts sped away from how I personally felt about being on television. The new thoughts flew to No-Eyes. This shift seemed to strike a swift blow to my psyche. What kind of messenger refused to give the message? What kind of messenger avoided opportunities to share the word of the message? What kind of messenger refused to take an opportunity to reach millions of people with her teacher's wisdom and knowledge about the future of human-kind?

These thoughts naturally made me think back on being with my sweet mentor. Mentally seeing her time-worn face, hearing her soft voice, feeling her gentle touch, brought it alive again. No, *she* wouldn't ever go on camera, but I was here to do that for her so that her words would be shared and spread so much further. If I didn't do this, would I then be in a position of failing her because of my own stupid shyness? Shouldn't I transcend my personal attitudes in deference to the greater good of sharing her prophecies and dire warning? Her hope for the future? Her Starborn-connected revelations? Oh, how I began to agonize over this. Seeing her in my mind again and hearing her gentle voice was as though she were sitting right beside me at my desk. Her soft whispers came as feather-soft breaths in my ear. To leave her message to the hands of fate or allow it to be dictated through word of mouth only was not in keeping with why she entrusted me to be her messenger to carry on after her. I was either a diligent student who did all she could to spread her teacher's knowledge, or I was a shy hermit who was afraid to speak out. I could make the work she left me to do either something wonderful or something hidden behind my own personal shyness. Couldn't I at least do this for *her*? Couldn't I at least give her all I could of myself in spite of myself? Were my own personal attitudes a greater issue than the work I came to do? Oh, how foolish I felt. I *could* do this for my gentle No-Eyes. Yes! I could!

And before my determination waned, I scribbled a note to Bob and faxed it off to him that night. I'd agreed.

In the morning I awoke to a sinking feeling. What had I done? Oh, God, what had I done to myself now?

Around noon Bob called. "You made my day! No! You made my year!"

Well. Yes, I was glad to hear that I'd made his year, but by then my nerves were twitching with anxiety over what I'd agreed to do. I listened to Bob go over the details for the NBC special. I listened to him explain that a woman by the name of Kathryn Kaycoff would be calling me. She was a field director for Greystone Communications, Inc. and they were doing the production work for NBC.

After I got off the phone I was nearly shaking. Now I had to talk to this field director of the production company. That sounded like scary stuff for someone who doesn't even like talking on the phone at all. Maybe that sounds like a wimp, but I love my woods—not the worldly aspects of life. I have Bill to take care of all that for me. I go out so little now that it's actually been since 1988 since I've pumped gas in any of our vehicles! The mountains have become my world where peace and true innocence of Grandmother Earth's pure essence has offered me solace and tranquility of mind and spirit. It's been this way for a long while now and, to emphasize how serious it had become, Bill recently commented that I probably couldn't make it out in the world alone now. I'd become too inexperienced interacting within it. He said I'd be like a kitten out on the interstate. Well! I sure don't believe that analogy is completely accurate, but I do know, vibrationally, I have a tough time whenever I do have occasion to go into Colorado Springs or Denver alone. The traffic makes me a nervous wreck and the static state of the overall atmospheric vibrations is like being continually bombarded by meteor showers.

These perceptions may sound more than a little over-sensitive, but nevertheless, they exist for me just the same. The world has, over time, become a less and less hospitable place for me to function well within. The more time I spend out in the forest within the boundaries of my protected Prayer Circle, the less time I spend participating in worldly aspects of life. This is not a conscious choice for me; it's nothing more than a natural evolution caused by the powerful draw of Grandmother's pure soul—Her high alpine mountains and sweet piney forests where all the true Innocents reside. This perspective—does it then make me a recluse? A hermit? I think not. Doesn't everyone attempt to reside where they feel best? Doesn't everyone strive to reach for wherever they'll feel most at peace? It is, therefore, within my ability to reside among the most beautifully harmonious and peaceful vibrations upon this planet. To choose otherwise would not be wise, for I must dwell among like vibrations in order to complete that which I came to do.

And so, this is how it was on the morning of the 26th. I, nervously attempting to take a tentative step out of my gentle wood to await the dreaded phone call from the production company's field director. I took deep breaths. I paced before the telephone. I wiped my sweating hands. Over and over I wiped them dry.

Finally I jumped when the phone rang. It was her. It was Kathryn Kaycoff.

Her voice was soft and her words were comforting. She'd been briefed by Bob. She knew of my shyness and stance on cameras. She said they could come up with a dozen ways to make me feel more at ease during filming.

I listened to her talk me through an explanation of filming details. She said that they were planning on hiring a husband and wife film crew out of Denver. We'd film wherever I felt most comfortable. We could do it in our house—such as my native room or we could go out into the woods. Ah yes, the woods!

We then talked for a while about my experiences and the books I'd written on prophecy. Kathryn made me comfortable and I was able to strongly emphasize how important it was for me to stress Hope in the interview. I told her how little I'd seen of hope being included in any prophecy program. I expressed how important it was for people to see a real balance between ill times and the hope that the beauty afterwards brings. She said that she'd make up some pages of questions to ask me and that I could interject anything I felt the need to get across to people. This sounded good because I had an awful lot to get across. I needed to stress the Hope people should have. I needed to convey vital information my Starman revealed to me regarding his People's upcoming interaction with humankind. I needed to be sure to include a variety of aspects and issues that no prophet or prophecy program had ever covered before now. I was filled with a building excitement to bring this beautiful balance to the usual negativity I saw today's prophets shouting out.

At the end of our conversation, I read her a little something I'd written after seeing a vision of the earth as if I were viewing it from the window of a space vehicle. I'd titled the piece, *Midnight Magnificat*. Kathryn thought that a visual of earth rotating among the stars with a voice-over of me reading the piece would make a beautiful ending to the program. After all, wasn't Hope what I was most interested in conveying? Oh, dare I believe that the program would or could end in such an uplifting manner? This then became my underscoring conviction that this project was meant for me to do. And before we concluded our conversation, we made plans to conduct the filmed interview on August 5th.

Placing the receiver back in its cradle, I sighed a deep breath of relief. Yes! This was one messenger who was going to give hope! No-Eyes' words of Hope were going to be the first whispers of It from among the many little doomsday-sayers out there. No-Eyes' whispers of Hope were finally going to be heard loud and crystal clear!

That night I went out into the woods to enter my Prayer Circle. That night I spent a long while giving deep thanks for the opportunity my shyness didn't manage to turn a deaf ear to. And my heart was overflowing with the warm and fulfilling sense of soon having the chance to give the world Hope.

The big day arrived. The birthing of August 5th was marked by brilliant sunrays spearing down out of a bright turquoise sky. I awoke and looked out the window. A wide smile matched the confidence-building one the dawn greeted me with. Yes, this was going to be a good day and I was more than ready for it.

Since Jenny and Aimee were now living and working up in Cripple Creek, Sarah was the last daughter left residing at home with us and she definitely didn't want to miss one minute of mom's filmed interview. She came with Bill and me to spend a day of high excitement.

The three of us rode into Woodland Park where we were to pick Kathryn up at the Hackman House Bed and Breakfast. Bill went up to the door and, when Kathryn followed him out, I was surprised to see that she looked like a high school girl dressed for a softball game. Her relaxed appearance served to put me at ease. Her easy mannerisms smoothed out any of my nerve endings that were left sparking with anxiety.

From the Hackman House we drove over to a convenience store parking lot where we'd arranged to meet up with the film crew. Sabrina and Tom Kargis were there waiting for us. Sabrina was in charge of the sound and her husband handled the camera work. We introduced ourselves and discussed various scenic areas where Tom needed to shoot what they called the "B-roll." I never asked, but I'm assuming that that means "background" filler film. I'd already chosen a serene spot that was along the road to our former Holiday Hills house. It was a place where there was a pond and I'd photographed it for my *Whispered Wisdom* pictorial book.

Tom had previously done some extensive Colorado photography work and was familiar with our region. He too had a few areas in mind and one of them was up our old Edlowe Road where the pond was. We didn't waste any more time talking about possible spots to shoot; we were already on the same track.

Once we reached the pond, we pulled off the road and Tom surveyed the banks with an experienced eye. He began setting up and showed me where to go. He came over to me and had me walk with him to mark the path he wanted to film. I was instructed to begin walking when he called to me.

I waited.

"ACTION!" he shouted from across the glistening pond.

I jumped and grinned. Action? The word brought an inner giggle. Gosh, he was making me feel like some actress when all I was doing was what I usually do—walk out from the woods. It felt odd. . .very odd.

I walked down to the pond and sat to write in my woodswalking notebook. As I sat there I thought how easy this was because I was just doing what I always did. I was being myself and actually forgot there was anyone else around.

Tom had me repeat the action several times so he could film it various ways. When we finished at the pond, I suggested we go up the road a bit to where we used to live. The second entry into Holiday Hills was the old road that Bill and I had walked. It had a wonderful view of the mountain road with Pikes Peak towering up behind it. We spent over an hour there filming Bill and me walking hand in hand together up the road. Other shots were taken of just me walking through the aspens.

With this B-roll concluded, we headed out to our Wildhorn house for the actual interview. We took a four-wheel trail up through our back property. We were high up by the time we stopped and I chose a spot where a fallen tree made a perfect place for me to sit. Pikes Peak could be seen behind me.

The crew began setting up their equipment.

Sarah was interested in seeing how the camera monitor worked.

Bill was excited and anxious for the show to begin.

I sat on the log while cameras were positioned, lighting checked and double-checked, and sound wired on me. I took some deep breaths. This was it.

I took a few more deep breaths in an attempt to calm my pounding heart and rapid respiration that constricted my voice. I thought I was ready.

Kathryn asked me a couple of basic questions as the film began to roll. The first serious question addressed the inquiry regarding what brought us to Colorado and. . .my nerves jammed my thoughts. I made a major mistake when I misspoke myself and Bill never caught it. Neither of us caught it until weeks later when we were viewing the entire interview video in our living room. In fact, we'd watched it three times before the mistake was noticed. I couldn't believe what I'd heard come out of my mouth and I asked Bill to rewind it to hear it over again. Yes! I had heard right. My heart sank. I'd said that No-Eyes appeared at the foot of my bed when it was really my dead grandmother who came to me that night. Oh God, I couldn't believe I'd said that. Do my nerves get so jittery that they scramble my thoughts that badly? What compounded the mistake was the fact that Greystone took that statement and created a re-enactment from it. This mortified me. Out of the hours-worth of taped interview, they picked the one time I seriously misspoke myself at the very beginning.

During the interview, I slowly became more and more at ease and found myself getting animated as I explained different aspects of an issue. Eventually the camera faded from my consciousness and my eye contact with Kathryn became an intensive focal point as I spoke of the great Hope No-Eyes emphasized with me for the mortals of this planet. I was feeling a bit playful when I spoke of the Starborn Ones and the new planet being prepared and how they were going to repair the damaging effects humans caused on this one. My eyes lit up when I stated that *the spirit was what survived and that was what people had to get in order now.* Such a simple fact that appeared to be so elusive to those centered on prophecy and preparations. At the conclusion of the interview, my final words were to read the *Midnight Magnificat* piece I'd written about the slowly rotating earth in space. When I'd spoken the last word, I looked up at Sabrina holding the microphone at my knees. Her eyes were misted. I looked over to Tom. He was silent. Kathryn just sat before the monitor. No one moved. Nobody spoke.

I lowered my head and put aside my papers. The interview was over.

"Your answers were great," Kathryn said, breaking the silence.

I smiled. "So were your questions."

I'd gotten so into the interview that I hadn't noticed that it'd gotten cold. At different times while I was talking, thunderheads rolled overhead and the sky drummed a threatening cadence. Now that I was out of the serious mode, I chilled to the breeze and went to the van for my serape.

Tom took the camera and suggested a few more action shots for the B-roll. I went into the woods and down a hill. He caught me off guard when I was returning. They'd filmed me after I thought they were done. Everyone thought that was funny to have pulled one over on me.

Returning to the house, Tom wanted a few shots of me reading in my native room. I didn't know he was going to have me actually turn a page or I would've also turned my head to the right-hand page as though I really was reading. I thought it must look a little strange to someone viewing those shots. The taping was now over.

Tom and Sabrina packed up and left. Bill, Sarah and I took Kathryn out to dinner. We went to a little local place at the end of our road. Oney's is a small, congenial place where the locals gather for pizza. One time when we were there, a regular customer came up to me and said that Carlos Castaneda was living in a cabin up the road and was wanting to meet with me sometime. We never did connect.

This night we had a good dinner and the conversation was warm and interesting. Kathryn gave her feelings about how the interview went. She expressed some ideas she'd carry out if she was the one who had control over putting the package together. We wished she'd had more of a say in that aspect of the production. Overall, the entire day went well and I didn't have any complaints or disappointments. Everyone was well pleased over how everything had gone. My interview tape was over two hours long. Greystone had volumes of information to utilize. Kathryn was happy because she'd made me at ease and she got a great interview. I was happy because I got so into it and spoke about so many different aspects of the future. . .especially Hope.

# AND THEN THERE WERE TWO

The middle of August brought us to a problematical point in our life. We'd approached a crossroads in respect to our decision on securing a new dwelling. Our buyer for the Wildhorn house still kept his offer valid and time was ticking toward the closing date. Of all the various properties Jane had taken us to, we loved the Four Mile Ranch cabin the best. The place was still on the market and we feared that it'd sell before we could secure it. This was the problem. We couldn't secure it until we were assured that our buyer was going to obtain the investors he was hoping to interest. Somewhere in the back of my mind, there lived a shadowy doubt that our buyer's offer would actually manifest into reality and this caused great concern. Although we could make a purchase offer for the cabin with a contingency clause, we felt that cabin was for us and were prompted to secure it in a manner that would preclude having to lose it if our buyer defaulted. On the 17th, we decided to lease the cabin for one year and then purchase it. That gave us time to sell our Wildhorn house if the present offer fell through. Though this was a way to obtain the cabin, it also was financially risky for us. However, we didn't feel we'd have to wait too long to find another buyer. We were optimistic and went ahead with the new plans while our current buyer bided his time.

On Saturday, the 21st, we moved out of the big Wildhorn house and into the small cabin. I'd previously sorted through all our belongings and given much of it away to friends and family. There was no way everything we'd accumulated could fit into the tiny place. Robin's furniture and belongings were already gone. We'd given pieces to Jenny and Aimee when they moved into their Cripple Creek house. All extra pieces left went by way of Giveaways to whoever could use them. I missed none of it. I wanted to get our possessions down to a bare minimum. I wanted the cabin to be simple.

Sarah's room ended up being the most troublesome as far as being able to contain one's belongings. She's a natural hoarder and had a lot of art supplies and sports equipment. We ended up putting her easel in a corner of our office—which was supposed to be the eating area. Her little closet was packed full and a good deal of her extra belongings went down in the walk-in space beneath the cabin.

We had an apartment-sized stacked washer and dryer in the hall closet. This took a bit of getting used to, but I ended up liking it a lot. When the weather was nice, I hung clothes out to dry. Overall, we managed to squeeze into the cabin space without experiencing any major crowding problems.

It seemed that we were presented with new surprises on a daily basis after we settled in. There were five little black squirrels that made it a habit of scampering up and down the pine tree beside the front windows. They'd wake us every morning by running over the roof. Their little thumping sounds became our alarm clock that was set for the squirrels' breakfast time. I'd get up and go into the living room and, there on the window ledge, the one squirrel I'd named Notch (because of a notch out of one ear) would be standing up on his back legs and peering in through the glass. He'd bob his head up and down, side to side, watching anxiously for me to prepare his breakfast. How funny it was to see him every morning. Company for breakfast was quite a treat, especially when we rearranged the living room and moved the dining table from in front of the fireplace to in front of those windows. We'd sit and eat our breakfast while Notch positioned himself at the window seat on the other side of the table. I'd fill his ledge with nuts and seeds and he'd eat right along with us. Eventually he came to eat out of my hand. I counted on his companionable presence every morning.

I don't believe I'd ever lived any place in the mountains where there were more kinds of wildlife around. Our birdfeeder was emptied before dinnertime each evening. A wide variety of birds began with breakfast and, what they spilled, the families of chipmunks, squirrels, and prairie dogs cleaned up. A fox family lived nearby. The deer and bear came to drink their fill at our small pond. Coyotes roamed and howled on our hillock after dark. Above, a great horned owl nested in the high boughs. Hawks soared the blue air current trails overhead. Life was serene—so serene and peaceful there. And Bill was finally able to come up from his depressive moods. Being out on the land and working on the Farm All tractor was a great help to him. He'd also had the use of a backhoe that the cabin's owner left behind when he returned to Florida for the winter. He'd offered it to us but we couldn't afford to buy it. The owner was leaving it until we actually purchased the property. Getting out and working the backhoe on various projects gave Bill something to put his mind on other than his black moods.

Around the end of August, we received our copy of Greystone's video interview. It was the raw, un-retouched copy. We were excited to see how it came out and, when we began playing it, I was absolutely embarrassed to see myself on video. It was the first time I'd ever been filmed on video. It was a strange feeling to be viewing oneself. Overall, once all the bloopers were edited out, we thought it made one heck of an informative piece that would end up being a two-hour interview. And, naturally, we wondered how much of it Greystone would end up using for the TV special. Only time would tell.

In September, when Sarah began her senior year, it became apparent that our new cabin location was too far from Woodland Park for her to be commuting. She was using our old blue pickup and it was eating gas like crazy, not to mention the wear and tear on that worn-out engine. When the snow flew, there was no way she'd be able to make it to school.

This situation was resolved by Robin offering her house in Woodland Park. She was only too happy to have Sarah come and stay with her and Mandy during Sarah's senior year. We tossed the idea over and discussed various details before deciding to accept her kindness.

Sarah was excited to make the move. Yeah, what senior wouldn't be thrilled to live away from mom and dad's eye for their last year of high school? So on a beautiful autumn day, we moved Sarah out of the little cabin and into Woodland Park where she took her first step away from the family nest.

Two days later, the offer to purchase our Wildhorn house fell through. The shadow of doubt that'd been lurking in the back of my mind solidified into a sneering monster that reared up and struck a major coup—on us. Now we had the monthly lease payment on the cabin *and* our house mortgage payment to make. We prayed that a new buyer would soon show up and, although this new situation would've normally caused us deep concern, our little piece of Paradise served to ease our cares and wrap its protective arms around our weary souls.

# COPS 'N' ROBBERS

Life for Bill and me at the small pine-sheltered cabin was serene and relaxed. He'd made comments that, since moving there, he'd felt lighter and hadn't experienced the blacker moods of depression that had come over him so often before. He was relaxing and enjoying the time spent outdoors when he'd ride the old tractor out the long drive and spend hours grading the rough dirt road that wound its curving way past a few neighbors' homes. It gave him a full-hearted feeling to once find a Thank You note tacked to our gate. It was from a neighbor who appreciated Bill's work on the road. Now you may wonder why that neighbor wasn't neighborly and didn't walk on up to our house to personally express her gratitude. Well, out in the more remote regions of the mountains, such as where we were, folks appreciate their privacy and don't go calling on neighbors very often, especially new ones that have No Trespassing signs nailed to their gate. People move out of the cities and into the seclusion of the mountains for various reasons, one being the desire for solitude and the peacefulness that comes with knowing one won't be bothered by others. Folks up here cherish these priceless treasures that define a unique way of life. Although we don't go chatting over the fence lines, we also are assured that we're there for each other if ever we're needed in any way. So the little note on our gate came as a warm greeting from our unseen neighbor who respected the unspoken neighborly mountain code of conduct. And Bill continued to putter that tractor up and down the country road in the autumn sunshine. Life was looking up. It was smoothing out. It was beginning to be good again.

Until. . .

On the morning of September 16th, our friend Frank called us and Bill answered the phone. Cuss words spewed forth. When I looked at him, his face became livid. When he hung up the receiver, his expression was one of disbelief.

"What's wrong?" I questioned.

"The Gold Rush was robbed last night," he said. "Jenny's *boyfriend* drove the *getaway* car."

Our peace was shattered.

Bill then called Aimee. "Where's *Jenny*?"

"I don't know," she said, "I'm real upset. We were robbed at the casino last night. I had to get customers out of the building while the robbery was in progress. I'm still shaking."

"Where the hell is *Jenny*?" Bill shouted into the phone.

"Probably down at David's," came the reply.

"Aimee! *David* drove the *getaway* car!"

"Oh God!"

Then Bill called David's house. A stranger answered the phone and exchanged a few words with Bill. Bill then relayed, "David's brother answered the phone at the apartment. He doesn't know where David and Jenny are."

Icy chills rippled up my spine. "Bill, David doesn't have a brother."

Time froze as we looked at one another. If David had no brother, who had answered his phone? What was going on?

And where in God's name was our Jenny?

Bill called the Cripple Creek police. The news was not good. I listened to Bill relay the information.

"David, his accomplice who did the armed robbery, and Jenny were picked up down at his apartment. They were taken to the Cañon City Police Station. They're being held until they're picked up and transported to Cripple Creek in a couple hours. No, David's nonexistent brother didn't answer the phone when I called—an officer did." He then repeated what he'd said to the officer about them being informed of Jenny's learning disability. The officer didn't see any reason why they'd hold her. We could pick her up as soon as they arrived at the station in Cripple Creek.

Oh, poor Jenny. How terribly distraught she must be right now.

We raced to the girls' house in Cripple Creek to await word of Jenny's arrival at the station there. Aimee's boyfriend, Robert, was at the house when we got there. He knew a few of the officers and was attempting to keep abreast of the situation. We paced the little house. Bill called the station again to talk to the detective in charge of the case. We were assured over and over again that Jenny was going to be released right away.

The phone rang. We could go get Jenny.

We hurried over to the station. There was a Denver TV van there. I worried if Jenny got on camera while they transferred the prisoners.

Charging up the stairs three at a time, we were met by the detective who was waiting for us in the hallway. Al Quintana said, "We're not releasing your daughter. She's going to be charged with conspiracy to commit armed robbery. She knows all the details and is being very cooperative. Her bail is set at one thousand."

*What!*

His words hit us harder than a Mack truck could've. I felt as though I were caught in the grip of a lucid nightmare that I couldn't extricate us from. It wasn't real. It wasn't happening!

Stunned, we returned to Aimee's house. We were completely dazed. We didn't have the thousand. Our two house payments took every cent we had. Aimee drove over to her bank and withdrew Jenny's bail money from her own savings. We were told that the prisoners would be transferred to the Teller County Sheriff's office in Divide around four o'clock. That's where we could post bail and get her out.

We waited and paced. . .paced. . .paced all afternoon. Just as we were about to leave for Divide, the phone rang. Robert picked it up. He was talking to detective Quintana. While Robert listened, he frantically motioned for us to get our butts over to the station. He whispered, "They're releasing Jenny! Get *going* before they change their minds again!"

So once again we rushed over to the station and charged up the stairs three at a time. Nobody was waiting in the hall for us this time. I pressed the intercom button. "I'm Jenny's mom. I've come to pick her up."

The door opened. Detective Quintana admitted us into the office where Jenny was sitting. She looked completely wiped out. She'd had no sleep last night and had been interrogated all day long. She rushed into my arms. Tears streaming down her face, she cried into my shoulder. "I'm so sorry, mama!"

Quintana talked to Bill while I held and comforted our scared and weary daughter. It appeared that they had to do what they did for a reason. They, in essence, used Jenny. They interrogated her all day. They got a lot of information about the whole scheme. Yet they could also clearly see that she had a learning disability and had no culpable part in the commission of the crime. She'd been cruelly manipulated and fooled by the perpetrators.

I told the detective that she shouldn't lose her job over this. He readily agreed and said he'd call her boss at the Gold Rush to make sure that wouldn't happen. He suggested that I go directly there to talk to her boss and maybe request a few days off for Jenny.

We put Jenny in our car and drove down the street where Bill pulled up in front of the Gold Rush. I went inside to talk to her boss. I was met by our friend Linda, who hugged me and led me over to Jenny's boss. Mark assured me that Jenny would still have a job and it was fine for her to take a few days off to recover from the experience. She'd been emotionally traumatized by the whole thing.

On our way back to our cabin where we were planning on caring for her, I asked Jen a question that I'd been puzzling over all day.

"Jenny, if you heard them planning the robbery, why didn't you tell your boss, or us, or Aimee? Why didn't you tell anyone?"

Her response was a typical one I could've predicted. "I didn't tell anyone because I thought it was all a joke, a game they were playing. I never thought they'd really do it. I never believed it was real."

Yes, I certainly believed that response. Jen was the sweet and innocent kind that could be so easily manipulated because of her complete trust in those she cared for. Never would she have considered that someone was lying to her.

When we reached the cabin we knew we had a rough road to travel. Jenny was absolutely heartbroken to know the love of her life lied to her and involved her in a serious crime. She was also emotionally shattered by the frightening day of intense interrogation she was put through. We spent many hours with her crying her heart out on our shoulders. Many more hours were spent trying to ease her new fear of the police.

Finally, our personal friend, Nick Adamovich, who was the Teller County undersheriff at the time, invited Jen and us to his house so he could help her out. We spent the afternoon there. He cooked us lunch and talked to her about a lot of related issues.

He was gentle with her as he explained the importance of completely avoiding David. Her first reaction was to feel sorry for him and want to visit him in the correction facility. Nick explained that doing something like that wouldn't look good for her and it could make the police re-think her status. Jenny was not one to abandon a love quickly. She loved deeply. She couldn't just turn it off and, for this, I loved her more than ever. Even though she'd been deeply hurt by the love of her life, she still had great compassion in her heart for him.

In time, Jenny went back to their Cripple Creek house and returned to her job. Because her heart had been broken so completely, she'd find herself working with tears filling her eyes. And her coworkers would hug her and give their full support. Her coworkers viewed her as family.

Some weeks later, a young man who also worked at the Gold Rush began taking Jenny out to dinner. He gave her warm support and comfort. Although Jenny insisted that this young Bill had no chance of becoming a serious boyfriend, she allowed herself to be given companionship by him. And, one evening, Bill brought Jenny over to the cabin. She handed me a large manila envelope. "Will you please burn this for me, mom?"

The envelope contained all of David's cards and letters. Jenny had finally cut the ties. And, by the look in her eyes when she looked in her new friend's eyes. . .she'd found someone very, very special.

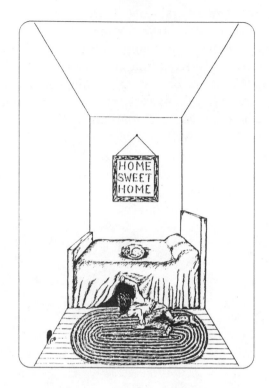

# REVENGE STRIKES A LOW BLOW

The robbery incident with Jenny plunged Bill back into his former melancholia. He was convinced that there'd always be one negative event after the other coming to plague our lives and, although he'd begun to really enjoy our little paradise in the pines, it no longer held the magic it once had for him. It appeared that his only joy in life was when he went into Woodland Park to see Cassie and submerse himself into his counselling sessions. The only other bit of joy he derived out of life was getting on the tractor and spending time outside on the country roads. I wasn't sure where I fit in anymore. I'd begun to wonder why our love or just being together didn't seem to mean as much as it once did; consequently, I was grateful that I was still able to derive much needed solace from the purity and innocence of nature. The woods never failed to give comfort and refresh my weary spirit.

. At the beginning of November, we were becoming concerned over Aimee driving the old pickup over snow-covered roads. She needed a more dependable and safe vehicle for all the long trips she took into Woodland Park and Colorado Springs from Cripple Creek. We decided to sell her our van for a dollar; we then passed the pickup on to Sarah who wasn't at such high risk driving it back and forth to school from Robin's house. This left us with my little Storm which Bill had to use for all his errands. I was again left without any means of transportation whenever he took off with things of his own to do, but being out at the cabin soothed any wanderlust I might have come over me. Even though Bill had lost his paradise perspective, I still held it close to my heart.

On Thursday, November 4th, nine inches of snow fell. Bill had an appointment in Woodland Park and couldn't manage to make it in with the Storm. We had another dilemma. He was upset over the fact that we no longer had a four-wheel drive vehicle to get us through the mountain winters.

His complaining got me thinking. I went over to the window and looked out at the little rollerskate-sized car. Large snow-flakes were falling. I turned to Bill.

"We really should have a four-wheel."

"No kidding," came the disgusted comment.

"Well," I added, "let's go get one then."

He turned to look at me. His expression was a defeated one.

"Last time I looked, it took money to buy a vehicle."

I grinned. "Maybe not."

The look remained. He hadn't been looking at all our options like I had.

"We can get another Astrovan without spending a penny."

He acted like my elevator finally stopped going all the way to the top. "You going to go steal one off the lot?"

I rolled my eyes. "All we have to do is lease one by using the Storm as the down payment. We wouldn't have to spend a penny that way."

His eyes widened. "What! But you love that Storm!"

"Yeah, I do." I sighed. "Let's get logical though. We need a dependable mountain vehicle and that little thing out there isn't going to get it. Every penny we have is going to hold onto the Wildhorn house until it sells. We can't afford to buy a vehicle. We *can* afford to lease one with a trade-in. That way we meet our needs without spending money we don't have. What's the alternative?"

He sat down. "Geez, honey, that'd be the second Storm you gave up."

"So?"

He shook his head. He shook his head while thinking my offer over.

I suggested he call our car dealer and get the particulars on trading in the Storm for a new van. He was on the phone and writing down figures twenty minutes later.

"Al says we could do it with no money needed. We could drive a van home today if we went down."

My eyes brightened. "See? Let's go do it then!"

He was acting reluctant.

I urged him on. "Why wait? The weather's getting worse out there. If we go right now we won't have such a hard time getting down there."

And we got in the Storm and headed down to Colorado Springs where he spied a new full-sized Blazer that he fell in love with. I didn't particularly care for it. It was too much truck for me. It felt like a man's vehicle. It was even too high for me to easily climb up into. Yet I didn't express my opinion because I could see how much he loved it. I hoped getting the vehicle would put a little happiness back into his life. That evening we drove back up the pass in the new Blazer. We drove back up in a blizzard that the little Storm would've been disabled in.

The Blazer seemed to lighten Bill's melancholia somewhat. He still had his days, but life was a little better. Generally things were looking up. I was glad I'd been able to offer my Storm up in order to see him happier.

By the time Thanksgiving came, we were doing much better. There had been no more devastating events to mar our life. That's not to infer that there weren't little things to irritate us, like the reader's letter that chastised us for having the Wildhorn house. This woman had actually gone out and seen it. She was completely outraged over its size. She claimed that I was only out for money and that she was going to try to ban my books from every bookstore in Colorado Springs because I was obviously a fake. What? She'd judged my books by what our house looked like? She passed judgment on me because she didn't know the facts? She didn't know that that house took three incomes to make its monthly payments. She didn't know that two families lived there. She didn't know that we had to sell it because Bill and I could in no way afford it on our own. People's penchant to judge out of ignorance never failed to pain me. I could not—no matter how hard I tried—understand such quickdraw conclusions. I suppose some folks aren't happy unless they can find something to complain about or criticize. Anyway, that night I prayed for that woman. I prayed that understanding and clear sight would begin to be a part of her thought process. I held no grudge, only compassion.

On Thanksgiving Day, we had a big dinner with all the traditional fixin's. The girls came over with their boyfriends and we had invited some close friends. Our table was full. It was full of the love and sharing between family and friends. This Thanksgiving sharply contrasted to the one the year before. That alone was something wonderful to be thankful for.

Christmas was equally beautiful. Again, the girls arrived with their boyfriends. Robin and Mandy were there. Our little cabin was filled with joy and happiness. As we were in the middle of the great commotion of opening our gifts, a neighbor knocked at the door. She'd brought us some wonderful bread and wanted to wish us a Merry Christmas. I tried to invite her in. I wanted her to share our merriment. She demurred, but looked about the raftered room and commented on how nice I'd done it up. She left then. After she was gone, I wondered if she'd spied the original artwork Carole Bourdo had done for *Soul Sounds* that hung over our fireplace mantle. I had the feeling she might have known who we were. We always go to great lengths to keep that quiet. Regardless, I wished she'd come in and had some time to share with us that Christmas Eve.

On Wednesday, December 29th, Aimee and Robert came over to visit. It was going to be one of "those" talks. We suspected that Robert wanted us to get to know him better. Aimee had talked about marrying Robert and we were expecting this son and in-law talk to be coming up.

The day was beautiful. The ground was blanketed with a fresh quilt of multi-sparkled crystals. Deer had slept overnight by the pond. Brilliant blue sky made a backdrop for the high-flying hawks that glided in pairs through their fields of crisp alpine air.

As expected, the talk was about getting to know Robert better. We were invited to ask anything we wanted about his past and his plans for the future. Actually, we didn't have many questions and we got into some interesting Starborn discussions, for Robert had had a memorable experience several years before he'd met Aimee.

As we were deep into the issue, the phone rang. I answered it and spoke to Jenny. She was in one heck of a dither.

"Mom! My money's gone!"

"What money?"

"The cash box I keep under my bed. It's not there!"

I sighed. Jenny was so proud of the money she'd been able to make on her own. She'd saved up over a thousand dollars of it.

"Did you look all over the house? Maybe you hid it somewhere else and forgot about it."

"No, mom. I always keep it under my bed. I had $1,100 saved up. Mom! That's all the money I have!"

"Is Bill with you?"

"Yes, and he's really upset I can't find my money. We've been looking all over the house for it."

"Well, look around again and call me back."

When I got off the phone, I asked Aimee about it. She confirmed that Jenny always kept her money in the same place and was very protective of it. Aimee kept hers in the bank, but Jenny kept her own money close by.

Aimee then had a heart-sinking thought.

"David's other two accomplices are out on bail. They were seen in Cripple Creek last week."

My stomach turned. "Do you think they got in and took Jenny's money out of revenge?"

Aimee was getting concerned.

Bill was becoming upset.

Robert was thoughtful.

I inquired of Aimee, "Did David know where Jenny kept all her cash?"

"Yes."

"Do you think he told his friends about it?"

Nobody knew the answer to that one, but it seemed like it wasn't an impossibility.

The phone rang again.

It was Jenny.

"Mom," she said through tears, "the money's not anywhere. We looked all over. It's not here!"

"Jenny, did David know where you kept your money?"

He did.

"Honey, do you think he could've told his friends?"

She didn't know.

"Did you know David's accomplices were out on bail?"

"Yeah, I knew. I was afraid they were mad at me for not going to jail like they did. Do you think they broke in and took my money to get back at me?"

I sighed. "Well, they probably needed money. And I wouldn't doubt that they could be upset that you got off so easily. Yet, Jen, they knew you didn't think the robbery was real, didn't they?"

"I guess," she sniffed.

"Honey? How well did you know these people?"

"Not very good."

"Do you think they'd be the kind to try to get back at you? Jenny, have you been afraid they'd try to contact you?"

"I don't know about the getting back part, but I've been afraid ever since I heard they were out on bail. I didn't really think about them trying to contact me, I was just afraid knowing they were out."

"Well, if you're positive that the money's not anywhere in the house, we'll come over and report it missing. Have you noticed if anything else is gone? How about your jewelry? Check to see if Aimee's blank checks are still on her desk."

"Now?"

"Yeah, honey, go look for me. Aimee's concerned about them." She came back a minute later. "Her checks are still there and it dosen't look like any of my jewelry's been touched. The only thing gone is my cash box."

"Okay, honey, we're on our way and. . ."

"Mom?"

"What, hon?"

"Do we have to call the police?"

"Yes, honey, we do. You have a missing cash box that had over a thousand dollars in it. We have to make a report. Don't worry. Remember, you're the *victim* again. Nobody's going to hassle you. Mom and dad will be right there in the house with you."

"Okay," came the weak reply.

Poor Jenny. She didn't want anything to do with officers again. She was still scared stiff of them.

Robert had to leave for an appointment elsewhere, so Aimee followed us up to Cripple Creek in her van. When we arrived, young Bill was extremely distraught over how upset Jenny was. Everyone was now suspecting that the robbery participants had taken their revenge out on Jenny.

We called the police and waited for them to arrive. When they did, one of the officers was familiar with Jenny. Jenny didn't like seeing this guy in her house. She was nearly shaking with anxiety.

The officers took the report. They examined all exit doors and the windows. Nothing looked jimmied or forced. One officer spoke alone with Jenny. Then he took Aimee aside and talked with her for a time.

What was suspected was an inside job. They suspected both girls and their boyfriends who had access to the house. It seemed that Bill and I were the only ones not included. What irritated me to no end was what Aimee said after the officers left.

"They think that the two accomplices somehow got to Jenny and threatened her into giving them her money. They think Jenny might have handed the cashbox over to them in order to protect herself from their threats."

I was outraged. "Jenny! Did these crooks contact you in any way?"

"No."

"Jenny. Look at me."

We made strong eye contact.

"You sure neither of them called here or came over? Neither of them stopped you on your way home from work?"

She kept eye contact and shook her head. "No, mom, I haven't seen or heard from them. Just knowing they were out scared me enough."

I believed her. If the bad guys had contacted her and threatened her into giving over her money, she'd be mad as a hornet. Jenny's just too stubborn to turn over her hard-earned money. She's too proud of what it represents—her great accomplishment at being self-sufficient. Everyone in the family knows how important that money is to her. It was like a big, shiny badge of courage that proved to her that she could make it on her own. No. No way she would part with that medal without one hell of a fight.

So then, the officers left the house with the feeling that Jenny was hiding something. We were left with feelings of complete helplessness. It was a draw. Nothing was ever heard of the money again. No follow-up from the police. No inquiries. No whisper of it. Only the sound of Jenny's crying.

# 1994

# GONE. . .AGAIN

The stolen cashbox had far-reaching effects in all our lives. Jenny was terrified to think that the freed gunman and his wife (who pretended to be a casino hostage for the robbery) had somehow gotten in their Cripple Creek house and taken her money in retaliation. She was constantly looking over her shoulder. She was living in continual fear.

Aimee too began jumping at shadows. She was sure the gunman had taken her sister's money. Who else could it have been? She knew *she* certainly didn't touch it. She knew Robert didn't. She knew young Bill didn't and nobody else had been in their house.

As a mother, I couldn't rest knowing how scared both my girls were. We had to do something to get them out of their house. Something, but what? Well. . .our own house offer had fallen through and it was now vacant—just sitting idle. To me, it was the only solution to the problem.

I approached Bill with it. "Bill? We'll have to move back into the house. The girls will be safe there with all of us together again and, besides, we can't keep paying on the house *and* this cabin. We'll have to terminate our option here."

He was aghast over my suggestion. "But you *love* it here!"

"I love our girls more. Their safety comes before any cabin."

So we terminated our cabin lease. The owner was very compassionate over the sad circumstances that forced us to leave the place he knew we loved so much. Sometimes compassion only goes so far—we lost the four thousand dollars we paid as the down payment.

In January, Jenny ended up quitting her job because she was still too scared to remain working where the gunman could find her. In January we moved out of our cabin and, the following day, moved the girls out of Cripple Creek. Their landlords threatened legal action until we showed our own real estate attorney the chimney photos we'd taken. We were all back together again at the Wildhorn house. The robbery was not only a tale of cops 'n' robbers and revenge, it ended up being the tale of Paradise Lost.

Before we moved out of the cabin, Bob Friedman at Hampton Roads had called to suggest the idea of me reading *Spirit Song* for an audiobook. I was a little reluctant at first, but thought I'd give it a try. Bob had a friend who was in the radio business and they wanted me to record some pages so they could hear how I read. If I did a passable reading, they wanted me to do the entire book unabridged. This was scary.

I got out our little tape recorder and began to read.

Chu-Chu barked.

I began again.

The phone rang.

I took the book and recorder into the bedroom. After reading three pages I listened to the result. I'd never heard my voice on tape before and it sounded strange, but the reading was okay.

I sent the tape off to Bob. The following week, he called to say that he and his friend, Cliff, thought I'd do a good job on the book. They made plans to schedule the reading at Get Reel recording studio in Colorado Springs. I'd already made arrangements for Carole Bourdo to read No-Eyes' part. She was thrilled and thought it would be a lot of fun. Until she said that, I'd been nervous and full of anxiety. Fun. Yeah, it'd be fun.

Shortly after we moved back into the Wildhorn house, we had Carole come over to do a little practicing. It was stiff going at first, but we soon slipped into a more accurate dialogue that was quick like the real No-Eyes and I most often conducted our interaction.

I'd spent a lot of time preparing our scripts. I'd photocopied two sets of the book and took a yellow highlighter to mark every spoken passage of Carole's. My lines were likewise marked. This, I figured, would make the actual reading go so much easier because only the actual words to be spoken stood out.

On Sunday, February 6th, Bob and Cliff arrived at the house. I fixed them an Italian dinner and Robin was over to give them a relaxing massage after their plane trip. In the evening, we talked about the recording procedure and listened to the sample music that my friend, Rick Burness, had recorded for the book. He'd done a great job and we were all well-pleased with his efforts. Rick only had a short time to put it together and get it to me in time. He was a real trooper and I'm ever grateful for his beautiful Giveaway to me.

The first day in the recording studio was Monday, February 7th. We were going to be there early; at least that's what we'd planned until when we were almost into Woodland Park I realized that I'd left my script at home. We turned around and retrieved it. I had Aimee call Bob at the studio to inform them that I'd probably be a few minutes late and why. When we got there, they were all grinning at the thought that I was subconsciously in denial over having to do this project. Denial? Nope, not me. I just wanted to get it over with.

It didn't take me long to get comfortable with the sound room and having the headphones on. Reading didn't go too badly either. One thing I really noticed, though, was what long sentences that Summer Rain author had penned. Deep breaths were required to finish more sentences than I'd like to admit to. After I made comments over the mike about that, those in the control room suggested I speak to the writer.

When it was time for No-Eyes to enter the dialogue, Carole came into the sound room with me and stood before her own mike. She was very nervous. Between us, we made some hilarious bloopers. We laughed and sometimes couldn't stop. Bob playfully threatened us with making a tape of the out-takes to sell. That didn't deter us though—we weren't proud—we were having so much fun we didn't care if a blooper tape was made or not. That first day we accomplished more of the book than was anticipated and everyone involved was feeling pretty good about how the recording was going.

On Tuesday, we sped through another third of the book. More bloopers were made. At times I was corrected for the pronunciation of certain words or coached on better ways to read specific passages in a more effective manner. At some of these times, I'd argue that that wasn't the manner that dialogue was originally exchanged, but I was a good little reader and followed Cliff's direction just the same.

When I walked in the studio on Wednesday, I knew the book would be concluded. I told Bob and Cliff to please let me read it straight through as long as I could still be articulate enough to be understood. I knew the reading of the ending was going to be one of the most difficult things I'd ever have to do. I knew I was going to relive it all over again. I knew the emotions were going to come pouring out again.

Before we broke for lunch that final day, while Carole and I were reading, we began hearing loud wind sounds in our mikes. Alan Blackwell motioned for us to stop and he came into the sound room to check out our mikes and the associated equipment. He and Cliff scratched their heads. No reason for the disturbance could be found. Carole and I continued.

Again the wind sound came.

Again the equipment was double-checked.

Again no technical reason for it was found.

Carole and I continued after the wind stopped blowing through our mikes. We read straight through until it was time for lunch.

I wasn't in the mood to eat that day. I was anxious to be finished with the ending of the book. I was eager to get the reading over with and hoped that I could manage it in one reading.

We returned to the sound room. Everyone was tense. There was the feel of expecting the unexpected. We were pleased that the recording was about to be finished, yet it was the finish that caused the most anxiety.

Carole and I read our parts and, when she no longer had any dialogue to read, she stayed in the sound room with me. I didn't want to stop for a break before the final pages were read. I wanted to go right on with it. And I did. By the time I got to the part where I parked the truck and stood on No-Eyes' porch, tears were beginning to seep from my eyes. I muffled some sobs while I read the part where I was walking through the empty cabin. The tears were pouring down my cheeks when I was looking out her window and remembering flying high with the falcon. I was reading and sobbing at the same time when I got to the last paragraph. The words were broken up and I looked out the glass to Cliff. He was checking with Bob to see if I needed to repeat the final words. Bob shook his head. Good.

They turned off their control room sound so I could have some privacy in my sorrow. It was so hard. I had just relived the experience of finding No-Eyes gone. It was so vivid and real—it was having her gone all over again. I never imagined it'd be so hard to read those last chapters. I never imagined I'd feel that she was actually gone. . .again.

When I left the sound room and joined the others in the control room, I was greeted with warm hugs. They all knew it'd been hard on me, yet everyone was thrilled with how well the entire recording had gone. Carole and I were done.

Thursday was reserved for Cliff, Bob, and Alan. They were going to spend the day putting it all together with Rick's music. Carole and I had a day off. I think we both needed it.

On Friday we were to all return to the studio to listen to the final version. From beginning to end we were going to hear how it all came together.

When I walked into the studio that morning, Bob had a

funny look on his face. Cliff turned to me and raised a brow. Alan was grinning. I couldn't imagine what was up.

Bob announced the revelation. "There are three blanks on the tape. They coincide with the places where the wind sounds were heard. We can't figure it because the tapes were stopped during the wind noise and they were running fine when the reading began again."

A shiver trembled through me. "What are you saying? What blank spaces?"

Bob tried again. "They're just three separate sentences spoken by No-Eyes to you. What's interesting is that just those complete sentences are blanked out—no fragments of sentences before or after are missing. Weird stuff."

I looked to Alan. "This kind of thing happens often with your taping sessions?"

His expression said it all. Never before.

I caught Cliff's eye. "So what's the explanation for these mysterious blanks?"

He shrugged. "Can't technically find a cause. It's odd."

Alan faced me then. "Ah, I really hate to ask you this, but you'll need to re-read those last lines. They're not quite audible enough."

I smiled. "That's okay, I can handle that."

He added. "We also need to re-do those blanks so we can cut them in."

"Which ones were they?"

He brought out the script and pointed them out. They were words spoken by No-Eyes that had definite meaning to me in the here and now. I had the strong impression that No-Eyes had actually interrupted our recording session to bring her words to my attention by making them blank and knowing they'd have to be repeated so they'd stand out. It was just like she was there speaking them to me.

One blank was my part. Just a single sentence where I'd said to No-Eyes: "That's because we're such good friends." By having me repeat that sentence, she was now emphasizing our close friendship. The second blank was extensive. Again, my part, where I was describing the spookiness of the cabin's altered atmosphere. This was when No-Eyes went from happy to extremely sad. This entire section had to be re-read by me and let me know that No-Eyes was currently sad over something about to manifest in my life. The final blank was Carole's part where No-Eyes said to me, "No can put head in dirt. Stuff come anyways. Summer no can hide. That not make stuff go away."

Carole and I did the readings over and they were edited in. Shortly thereafter we were sitting on the couch in the control room listening to the audiobook from beginning to end. At different times during the day, different listeners arrived. Sarah came down right after school to hear some of it. Robin and Mandy arrived to listen until the end. By dinnertime, we'd heard the entire tape and were pleased with how well it turned out.

During the final chapters of the recording, Bob's friend Maria came in with her friend. Maria had had previous discussions with Bob regarding her video taping an hour-long interview with me about the Changes. She had television connections and could get it on PBS. She also wanted to do a Spanish version. Bob had made arrangements for the five of us to go out to dinner after we were finished at the recording studio. I was not eager to discuss doing any more video interviews after the NBC fiasco and how they'd not included much more than my name, much less mentioned any of the words on Hope for the future. I'd been so disgusted that I foreswore cameras forever after.

At dinner, I was hoping the subject of Maria's planned project wouldn't come up. I was wishing for a relaxed dinner after having just completed three full days of recording. I was wrong. Maria couldn't resist bringing up the issue of her video and why wouldn't I want to jump at the chance to have my say? She assured me that I could have some control over what was said. She agreed that I should speak of Hope for humankind and the earth. She expressed how much she wanted to make a balanced piece that wouldn't put so much fear and hopelessness into the hearts of people.

I listened to Maria. Her friend also gave input supportive to her cause. I listened, but didn't agree. By the time we parted in the lobby of the Antler's hotel, I hugged her after expressing how hard camera work was for me and that I just didn't think

I'd be doing her project. She smiled and told me to think about it a little more. I put it on the back burner.

Saturday evening, Bill and I picked up Cliff and Bob at their hotel. We drove them out to Carole's house. We'd all been invited for dinner. When Carole invites you to dinner, you're out of luck if you can't make it—she's an absolutely fantastic cook, especially when she prepares the salmon she catches when she visits her daughter Lauri in Alaska. Carole's a great fisherwoman!

The evening at Carole's was warmed by the pine logs snapping in her fireplace and the friendships we'd forged between those sitting around it sipping wine. Her dinner was wonderful and the conversation afterward was just as good. Taking new people over to Carole's is always an exciting event for me because her place is so unique. She has the most interesting nature things. Whale spine bones personally collected off a beach in Mexico. Huge, comfortable chairs made out of enormous stumps and branches; these, covered with beautiful and lush sheepskins. She has the most unusual native items I've ever seen. And such one-of-a-kind nature articles that I want to just stay there forever. In her studio is an enormous set of moose antlers that she lugged back from her last Alaska art show. Her daughter Lauri teased me that I could have a set just like it, but only if I drove up there to get them. She's always trying to entice me up to Alaska. . .I just might take off for there one of these days.

After we dropped Cliff and Bob off at their hotel, we drove back up the pass in a lightly falling snow. We were glad we had the Blazer because, by the time we were headed toward Florissant, the blizzard got so bad we could hardly see where the road was. Cars were pulled off onto the shoulder all along the way. The only way we could manage to make it home was to shut off our lights as the other trucks were doing. Driving without lights stopped us from being blinded by the brilliant white snow that was driven against the windshield. We were relieved to pull into the garage. We were relieved that the recording was over. We were relieved to have decided not to do any more interviews or publicity. We needed some peace.

# STALKING THE ELUSIVE SUMMER RAIN

The remaining days of February were inundating me with publicity issues. After the NBC special was aired, I'd received various other requests for interviews or appearances. I didn't want anything to do with such things. It was hard enough to speak before a camera without having the most critical aspects of my message edited out. What I found was that the film people only went after the most devastating predictions; they weren't in the least interested in the idea of hope or renewal. I suppose that's the boring stuff to them. I suppose they have the right to pick and choose what they want to take out of a person's interview, but that's only proven to me the futility of trying to get a balanced and complete message out about the Changes. Gloom an' doom is all these people are interested in. Gloom an' doom sells. Hope doesn't. And so it was that I refused to participate. I didn't like their game and I didn't want to play.

So the remaining days of February were spent turning down interview inquiries coming to Hampton Roads. By March and well into that month, Maria was still working hard on convincing me to do the video. She played on my sympathies by explaining how little the Spanish-speaking people get of the subject of Earth Changes. She said they had a right to be made as aware of the future as the rest of the world was. She reiterated the fact that I could approve of her project outline and make suggestions if I wanted. She said we could arrange the actual filming in any way that was most comfortable for me. We could be walking in the woods, sitting on a ridge, curled beside a roaring fire in my native room or at any other place I thought I might like to be.

Although Maria was convincing in her arguments, I still maintained my former stance. I didn't want to do any more videos. No more interviews. No more publicity. No more cameras.

Bob attempted to convince me otherwise. He'd met with Maria to discuss my message and how well a video interview would do for the Spanish people. He was also thinking of offering the English version to my readers. Well, yeah, here was a marketing possibility. That alone made Maria's project attractive to him. But to me, I just didn't care about that kind of thing. The way I saw it, *Phoenix Rising* and *Daybreak* covered most of what I had to say on the subject. Making a video of it was redundant except that there'd be a Spanish version that would reach a lot more people.

Maria reached me by mail. She'd sent me the project outline that detailed how film of disasters would be cut into the interview. She set aside a portion of the script for my pet issue—Hope. She hoped I'd be amenable to how the video was going to be done. In her letter, she gave me the opportunity to suggest changes or add any ideas I might come up with. I had the feeling that I was being tempted with a juicy carrot. Yet the carrot appeared to be a palatable one. The outline was done in a balanced manner. The project appeared to be a viable one that would allow me to finally get the needed balance across to the public.

I read and re-read the project outline. I thought long and hard on it. I meditated. I looked into the Vision Smoke. And I went out into the woods late at night hoping to get some clarity from owl and cougar. But they weren't showing themselves yet. They'd not showed themselves since we first moved into that cursed Changeling House. They were keeping their distance. I was on my own. So, so alone for so long.

Eventually my compassion for the Spanish-speaking people won out. That was the only aspect of Maria's argument that I couldn't counter effectively. It was for this reason alone that I finally agreed to do her video.

Bob was excited.

Maria was relieved.

I was accepting—I was accepting of facing the camera's big eye once again.

As the early spring days passed without event, several other requests for interviews came in. I avoided them all. I refused to even find out the details. I planned on doing Maria's project and that was all I was going to do.

Publicity people and those interested in including me as the focal point or addition to their projects were not the only folks looking for me. Reader interest had spread by this time. Having so many books in print sparked a renewed surge of people seeking me out for various reasons. Some found a few of my friends and attempted to find me through them. Some wrote letters marked URGENT in the hopes of getting my attention to connect with them. Others claimed life and death situations or that their guides told them we had to meet. I've been followed. I've been searched out. I've received more threatening letters, real sick ones. Yet I still remain the same simple, mountain person I've always been. I still avoid publicity whenever possible. I still perceive myself as being no more important than the next woman in line at the grocery store. I'm still me. And I still have a hard time understanding why many see me otherwise. I just want to maintain my mountain life where the most comfort and wisdom is still found within the piney critter-filled woods. Avoiding publicity or people is not a clever move to appear mysterious nor is it proof of an arrogant personality. Avoiding publicity and notoriety is inhercntly natural to me. I don't want to stand out in a crowd. I don't want to be recognized everywhere I go. I don't want folks treating me as being someone special or different from them. I never wanted that when I agreed to write the books and, after all these years, I still don't want any part of it. I've never stopped being me. Me is all I strive to be.

# LAST CHANCE FOR HOPE

While Maria was busy working on other projects before getting to her video on me, I had a little breather time that was free of publicity inquiries. This, I hoped, was a sign of things calming down. It wasn't.

On Monday, April 4th, Bob called. He talked with Bill. Bill got off the phone and came downstairs to my desk.

"Bob just called."

I looked up at him. "Oh? What he'd have to say?"

"Denver's Channel 4 News wants to do a three-part series on prophecies. They want a segment on you."

I smiled. "They do, do they."

Bill didn't find it as amusing as I did. "I think you should think about it."

"Why?"

"Because it's a great chance to get some of your message out. The NBC special gave you three minutes out of two hours of interview they could've used on you. The Denver news can get you more than that."

"So? What's the use if all these television people want is gloom an' doom? What's the use if all they want is over-dramatized displays of spectacular devastation. These people don't want to hear words like renewal and hope. Give me a break, Bill. I've learned my lesson the first time around. I'm not interested in making the same mistake twice."

He heaved a heavy sigh. "Look, will you at least consider calling the news reporter and talking with her? It can't hurt to get a fix on their plans and a feel for what they want to project to their viewers."

I didn't agree. "Why would it be any different? It's still NBC. You think just because it's local and not national that they'd give a little extra TLC to a local author? I don't think so. I don't think so at all. It'll be no different than before. Once they get the interview in the can, they pick an' choose just like all the others. I'm not interested. Call Bob and let him know my decision." I paused. "Gosh, Bill, you'd think he'd know how I feel after seeing how *Ancient Prophecies* zeroed in on a couple of No-Eyes' gloomy statements."

Bill went back upstairs. Bill didn't call Bob back. Bill wanted to wait until he worked on me a little more.

Eventually my own thinking brought me around to a reversal. I thought a lot about the recording studio and the mysterious happening that appeared to be caused by No-Eyes herself. What did she really mean when she emphasized that I "couldn't hide"? What was "gonna come anyway"? Was it publicity that I needed to do? Was she telling me not to hide from it? This is what I interpreted her words to mean. This is the only reason I reversed my decision. I called the Denver reporter.

By talking to Thelma, I was again put at ease with their projected plans. They definitely *wanted* some balance to the NBC special. As a local news program they wanted something more than devastation and sensationalism. They were looking for something good in the region's future, something for people to look forward to. And Thelma seemed excited that she'd found someone who could give that message to their viewers.

On Monday, April 11th, Thelma and her cameraman met Bill down at the Fossil Inn in Florissant. They followed him up to the house. We talked for a bit and I had fresh sweet rolls and coffee for them while they watched the entire raw Greystone interview. Before Thelma interviewed me I wanted her entirely familiar with my message so she could arrange her questions accordingly.

Watching the Greystone video, the cameraman became increasingly irritated. He didn't like how the NBC interview had been filmed. Every time I was interrupted, he sighed and groaned. "I won't stop your interview when we do it," he promised.

After the video was finished, we talked about the material it covered. We talked of Rocky Mountain changes, the difference Starborn intervention will make, future technology, lasting effects of geologic alterations, etc. Then we went upstairs to my native room where I sat in my chair and waited for the cameraman to set up his lights and equipment.

The interview itself didn't last long, but the information covered was balanced. I'd finally had a last chance to give the Hope I'd been so desperately trying to convey. After the interview, film was taken of me writing at my desk. When all was finalized, Bill and I took them out for lunch at the local spot nearby. Oney's was crowded at the time, but we enjoyed the meal and the conversation that went along with it. Overall, we thought I'd made the right decision to do the interview.

A few weeks later. . .it aired.

No word of Hope was whispered.

Hope wasn't a part of the program content.

Hope didn't exist. Neither did my trust in interviews or an interviewer's word. I felt like a little mountain fool who was stupid enough to believe what the big city person said. How sad to feel a fool for trusting another's given word. How very sad.

And so it was that my last chance for Hope had come and gone unsatisfied. Yet. . .I still thirsted for the one opportunity to make that my main message. I still thirsted for that. And though I thought myself the stupid little mountain fool, I believed myself fool enough to keep on hoping. That kind of fool never completely gave up. Maybe Maria's video. Maybe.

# REVELATIONS DENIED

In the evening of April 11th, Bill and I reviewed the day. We thought the Denver news interview had gone well. We held out hope for it. The hour was late when he noticed how tired he was and went up to bed. I sat and thought on various issues in our life. All was not entirely peaceful. Bill still experienced periods of deep melancholia and was often on the telephone in private conversation with a new friend who had come into our lives. I had no problem with their frequent marathon discussions because I figured that, if I couldn't help him maybe another could. It appeared that he felt I was seriously lacking in areas he believed he desperately needed fulfilled. He'd expressed that he still carried a deep heart pain that I didn't understand and wasn't able to ease for him. He felt the love I had for him within my heart was blocked from flowing out so he could feel its energy touch him. I didn't understand that concept. I thought the love in one's heart was a warm, pulsing fullness of light that quite naturally radiated from the entire body. He said it had to flow like a channelled current when we hugged—that current had to be felt by the other. Maybe I wasn't doing it right; all I know is that my love radiated out from my entire being and I couldn't manage to contain it in a channelled kind of directed flow. Since he couldn't feel this from me, he believed I was emotionally dysfunctional and had blocked my love for him. Consequently, because he said he couldn't live without feeling this emotional flow of pure love, he was compelled to seek it elsewhere. He said that flow was the only thing that could heal his heart pain that remained from Vickie's initial rejection of him and God back in 1991. I was at such a loss as to what to do for him. It seemed I couldn't help in any way other than to accept whatever avenue or whoever he believed could heal his pain through the emotional transfer of love. And so I accepted this situation, a situation that saw him turn to another and leave me behind because I wasn't emotionally satisfying for him. Much later, toward the end of the year, I also discovered that there were various other aspects he felt I was seriously lacking in. I suppose this makes me the cause of his problems, I don't know. I don't know because he never complained about me before Vickie came on the scene. I just don't know. But I did know that our new lady friend seemed to fit his criteria and I sat back to let her do all she could to help him heal his heart pain even though, all the while, I felt very alone and unloved.

These thoughts on our life shifted to life in general. I began thinking of humanity and all the deep and real sorrows people are forced to suffer. The hungry mothers in Third World countries who have no tears left to cry while trying to feed their starving, emaciated babies with dried-up breasts. I thought on those in war-torn lands who were forced to flee barefoot with their meager belongings on their backs. I thought of the homeless street people who curled up on park benches. I thought. And I thought until all the vivid visuals weighed upon my weary mind and drove me upstairs before the fireplace in my native room. There I sat before the gently burning fire and meditated until all the sad images had faded.

I have no way of knowing how long I remained in the meditative state, for I'd not glanced at a clock before entering it. When I came into full awareness once again, my Starman was sitting before me in my reading chair. I was startled to see him, for we hadn't had any physical communication since moving out of the Holiday Hills house.

Though I was excited to set eyes on him again, his own demeanor was one of seriousness. I took the cue and waited to find out what he came to reveal. I wish he'd never appeared.

Our visit was not a conversational one—it was instructional. The instruction was based on the subject of reality and humankind's origination. The revelations were profound. They contradicted much of what earth mortals currently believe regarding their beginnings. They contradicted aspects of the Bible and most religious teachings and belief systems. They tied in Starborn activities since the beginning of time and this aspect directly connected with most miracles and apparitions of saintly figures throughout history. His revelations detailed how the Ten Commandments tablet was technically engraved, how Moses' burning bush didn't actually burn, how the Red Sea was really parted. He identified Jesus' true genealogy and what the brilliant Christmas Star really was. He identified the true source of the Voice that came to Abraham and Moses. The subject of spiritual messengers was detailed in precise terms. And how humankind had gone so far off the mark by making gods of them and, in turn, creating religions of their new gods. He emphasized how the *Word* was all that was ever meant for humans to hold onto and uphold—not the physical messenger who came bringing the Word.

My Starman also spoke of No-Eyes. This, more than any other words that came from his mouth, plunged me into a deep despondency. It was pointed out that she didn't reveal certain facts to me during our times together. No-Eyes, being in routine contact with the Starborn, felt it best to take me only so far, thereby teaching me the Truths in stages. She was one stage and my Starman was the second. In No-Eyes' stage, I was shown how compassion, prayer, and pure love could change the world. I was led to believe that that meant the earth after the Changes. . .an assumption. I was led to believe that Hope was paramount for people to hold onto as their greatest saving grace in respect to viewing expected upheavals. . .an assumption. And I felt betrayed. I felt betrayed when my Starman showed me a brand new and pristine planet that a messenger will carry Grandmother Earth's spirit to. And this beautiful planet was what I saw in my Midnight Magnificat vision. I thought I was looking at our earth. . .I was not.

Five years prior, a major revelation was given to me regarding the critical time frame we're living in. This is the most unique one ever experienced because it's a precise parallel that is finely calibrated to balance out the time of Jesus. Starman said that Jesus was not actually God's son, but rather the Male Aspect of God in physical form. Sometime during this concluding time frame, God will send His *Female* Aspect to bring the balance full circle. An *"only* son" God has not. . .but God does have Male and Female Aspects. My Star friend said that God initially sent one of His aspects which mortals called "Son" and then He will send His balanced aspect which mortals will erroneously call "Daughter." The correct distinction must be maintained. All mortals are sons and daughters of God, but only once will He create a physically manifested Male and Female Aspect of Himself upon this earth. And the experiences of both follow the balanced parallel of each other, only this time, *Belief* will be deemed to generate not from the understanding and utilization of high physics (miracles and holograms), but through the people's inherent recognition of Truth. That will be the paramount criterion this time around. Not through the sighting and witnessing of awe-inspiring miracles, but through the clear perception and inner recognition of Truth.

My visitor spoke of many other subjects that related to the reality of Reality. One such aspect was how their simply created holograms are utilized to inspire religious beliefs and bring about a greater depth of faith among humankind. He smiled to say that several apparitions of the Virgin Mary will occur simultaneously in different regions of the world to prove this. He detailed how effectively his Star relations borrow a belief system's images of religious figures to instill a return to spirituality and the Word. This, he emphasized, was to rekindle prayer.

Many more aspects were spoken of as I listened and remembered bits and pieces that came to the forefront of my mind. Yet what struck me personally was his bringing up the issue of my recording session. The blanks—what was said during those blanks—that had to be repeated. "Summer no can hide. Stuff gonna come anyway. Summer no can stop stuff." The "stuff" No-Eyes was referring to was the reality of Reality that my Starman was now revealing to me. No-Eyes was telling me that we were still "such good friends" and that she was "sad" for what new Truth I'd learn from my Starman. She knew I'd feel betrayed by her. She knew she wasn't showing me the whole picture. She couldn't show me the complete picture because it wasn't time and I wasn't ready to see it. Now everything was perfectly clear. Now I came into the wisdom of her words that broke through on recording day. Now I too carried a heavier burden.

After my visitor left I felt a great weight upon my shoulders. I thought long and hard about all he'd said. Each fact was taken and seriously looked at. I turned them around and saw all angles. I flipped them upside down and then viewed them from various vibrational frequencies and dimensional shifts. Each one came up pure. Each one glistened and threw off brilliant rays of all their facets. . .each facet a sparkling crystal. It was then I knew all my friend had said was true. It was then I wondered how I could ever share such a profound message. And I grieved over the burden passed onto me. I grieved over the knowledge I was tempted to deny.

# TRACKS OF THE COUGAR

The far-reaching ramifications of my Starman's visit had profound effects on me that linger still. Yet, while they were so fresh in my mind, I found myself caught in a swirl of emotions that began with feelings of betrayal and ended with a great welling of purpose. And, after giving many days' worth of deep contemplation to all the different aspects involved, I clearly saw the direction my new path led to. . .the new *altered* future. As No-Eyes emphasized during the recording session—I couldn't hide from it, it was going to come anyway for me. And I also clearly saw that this new trail precluded any more media publicity. All the puzzle pieces fit so perfectly now. The new scene was revealed.

One bright April morn, Bill greeted me with a message. "No more media for you."

I wasn't surprised by his words. The subject matter—or at least portions of it—sometimes found its way into Bill's mind too.

We discussed some of these that he was aware of. We agreed with the logic of them in light of what we'd just learned, especially the admonition for me to stay clear of any UFO documentaries that I may be invited to participate in. We also talked about our misinterpretation of No-Eyes' message in the recording studio. Now it made a lot more sense, although, personally, I still had to deal with the issue of earth's future being altered.

After we talked, Bill went out the door. He was on his way to pick up the mail. He came right back in.

"Hey, everybody! Come to the front door!"

Jenny, Sarah and I scrambled from different parts of the house to see what he wanted.

Bill pointed to the deck planks. "We had a visitor."

Large, muddy grey cougar prints went from the front door and trailed back to the picnic table on the deck.

We followed them.

Two forepaws went up on the picnic table seat where he'd reached with his mouth to steal away an elk jaw I'd been drying in the sun.

"He stole my jaw!" I cried in amused amazement.

Bill looked at me. "Guess he came to mark the *end* of your *talking*. There's no more cameras for you."

I was stunned by the message. I whispered, "No more media."

We then took photographs of the grey pawprints. What was particularly interesting was the fact that the prints *began* at our front door. None were found on either of the two long stairways leading up to the high deck that was forty feet off the ground. If the cougar leaped up, there'd be at least one set of smudged prints where he landed with a forceful forward pounce. Every print was perfectly formed. Every print was equally clear. Wouldn't they become less distinct—less muddy—as he walked about the dry deck? Was this a real cougar? In our hearts we knew the answer. In our hearts we knew my companion had come to underscore my special friend's words and verify my new direction.

On Friday, April 15th, Bob sent us a fax. He informed us that a company in Virginia Beach was putting together a television special based on UFO experiences and I could be a part of it if I wanted. He said that it'd be a possibility for me to even play myself if that sounded interesting.

In light of my Starman's recent revelations, I had to call Bob back and briefly give a perfunctory explanation why there was no way I could accept participating in such a project. I told him I'd compose a detailed letter that he must keep confidential and destroy when he was finished reading and thinking over the content.

And this is just what I did. It was seven pages long. It shared some of the revelations my visitor had given me that night and it gave one profound reason why Bob must not consider me for any UFO projects in the future. After he read the letter he completely understood my new position.

I'd also informed him of my new position on media publicity and that the Starman's information would then keep me from doing Maria's video on the Changes, for the Changes had drastically changed. I could no longer look someone in the eye or face a camera with any integrity in my soul if I spoke of hope for saving earth. I was informed that there was only one way this could be manifested, but I couldn't speak of that aspect either. My mouth was silenced. What I *could* say would be too incredible for those walking within this time frame to accept. That left me with nothing to say. . .at least not until the time was right.

On Monday, April 18th, we invited our friend Jane over to list our house again. We felt we'd reached the right timing for it to sell. We'd gone through many transitions in this house and the appearance of the Starman and cougar signalled us forward. We lowered our asking price and anticipated a fairly quick sale. On the 21st, a man from California flew out to see it. An offer to purchase came on the heels of his visit. We were set to close on July 11th.

So then we needed to get busy looking for something else to move into. Something smaller, yet semi-secluded. Something much cheaper. Something out of the area we'd been in for so

long. And Jane showed us a house on May 7th that left no
doubt in our minds that it was the one meant for us.

We were met at the door by the seller's real estate lady's
assistant, Lisa. She showed us around and then Bill and I began
wandering here and there independently. While Jane and I were
inside, Bill called to us from the deck where he was standing
with Lisa.

"Mary! Jane! Come out on the deck and *look* at something!"

What we looked at was each other. We had questioning
frowns on our faces. We went out on the deck.

Bill was grinning like a Cheshire and pointing up to the
sky.

We looked.

An enormous double rainbow encircled the sun. Two rings
of rainbow colors were separated from each other by a brilliant
blue inner sky that was far clearer than the rest of the sky
outside the outer ring.

Lisa looked to me. "Mary! What does it mean?"

Her question startled me. Did she knew who I was? Usually
I always assume that people don't know I'm Summer Rain.
She didn't mention my books so I figured she was just wondering if I had a feel for the heavenly sign. Later I found out
that she really didn't know who I was but was shocked to find
out later and disappointed that she didn't realize it when we
were together on that deck.

The four of us stared at the double rings for a long while.
Jane and Lisa ran to their cars to grab their cameras. The rings
were so wide and huge that the entire circle couldn't fit into
the frame. They had to take top and bottom halves of it.

We all had feelings that it was a sign sent to verify the
rightness of the house. Lisa joked about it. Jane nodded her
head and grinned. Bill and I wondered.

The house had a completely different setting than what I'd
planned on locating. It sat high up on a ridge and, looking down
from the deck, you watched the Rocky Mountain sheep prance
on the rocks below. It was a "see-to-forever" view and I knew
Bill loved it. Its sunny location provided the house with passive
solar energy and the big windows gave an incredible panoramic
view of the mountains. This was it. He loved it.

Me? I liked it a lot. I liked it, yet it wasn't woods.

We drove back to our Wildhorn house and wrote up an offer.

It was accepted.

# BIG HEART DAYS

May and June were hectic months. We not only had packing to do, we had Sarah's high school graduation to attend and then prepare for Aimee's wedding. These two major events served to take Bill's mind off his heart pain and lift his mood for a while. Watching your daughters reach high points in their lives was a wonderful reason to rejoice and laugh at the tickle that a full heart gives within one's chest.

On Monday, May 23rd, Bill and I drove Sarah over to the Woodland Park High School where the senior's Capping Ceremony was to take place. We were so proud of her high grade point average and how determined she was to keep it up there. She'd expected a lot of herself and worked to manifest that expectation. Now came the time that made it all worthwhile.

When her name was called, she stood and walked up to the

front of the auditorium. Mom followed on her heels and, when four others joined us, we crowned our daughters with the sign of their accomplishments. Having the mushy heart that I do, tears misted my eyes as I set the cap on Sarah's head. How embarrassing. I'm always embarrassing myself with such extreme sensitivities. Yet the event was one that she and I shared with full hearts.

The following Saturday was graduation. Bill and I took a lot of pictures. I wasn't sure how well mine would turn out because, when I looked through the viewer to focus, everything was always blurred. Between us we ended up with great photographs of the entire event. What brought an amused moment to the ceremony was when Sarah's name was called and the drummer gave her a thundering drumroll. It would be no mystery to guess what instrument her boyfriend plays in the band. Jeff didn't miss a chance to show who he was rooting for. After the ceremony, Sarah spent the day with her friends at Jeff's house and we returned home. The rest of the month and most of June, we focused on Aimee's upcoming wedding plans.

The big day for Aimee and Robert was on a Thursday. They both had June 23rd off from work and had decided to begin their life together on that day. The date was also an open one for the quickly-booked location at which they'd planned the ceremony.

Aimee stayed overnight at our house on Wednesday and, come Thursday morning, the place was ringing with excited voices and a flurry of activity. I helped her get dressed and took a lot of pictures. Robert's sister had gifted Aimee with a limousine ride for the women in the family and it looked quite out of place driving up our long wooded drive. The driver opened the door and in climbed Jenny, Sarah, me, and Aimee.

What a thrill the girls got out of the ride. They looked about them in total awe and were amazed to see an aquarium filled with swimming goldfish extend the length of the side windows. Jenny played with the radio and Aimee spoke through the microphone to ask the driver to please make a stop at City Market before heading down the pass to Green Mountain Falls. What a kick the girls got over getting out of a white limousine in front of the grocery store. Jenny had to run in and pick up some film. Sarah went with her and a few of the cashiers who knew Aimee were shocked to find out who was sitting in the parked limo. Me? I felt very much out of place after being used to pickups and trucks. Yet it was a little amusing to sit in the luxurious vehicle with Aimee and look out through the darkened glass to watch people's curious expressions as they passed. Ah, if they only knew it was only us sitting in that ritzy thing.

When we arrived at the lake, most of Aimee's guests had already gathered on the island and the harpist was comfortably situated in the shade of the gazebo. Aimee and I stayed in the limo after Jenny got out to stand beside her young Bill, and Sarah met up with her waiting Jeff. The two couples were going to precede Aimee across the bridge to water's edge where the ceremony was to take place. Bill had driven Robert from Florissant to Green Mountain Falls. I suppose the father of the bride wanted to make sure the groom showed up. Well, that was just a joke we were lightly passing around, but Robert did ask Bill if maybe they could stop off at a few bars on the way down the pass. That too was a standing joke between them.

Everyone was there. And when Aimee spied Robert all dressed in his classy tails, tears started running down her cheeks. "Oh mom," she exclaimed, "Robert looks so handsome!" I smiled, agreed, and gave her a tissue. We stayed together in the vehicle until Robert had escorted his two young boys over the bridge and situated the three of them in front of the nondenominational lady minister who was also a shamaness. When Robert and the boys turned to face the crowd, Aimee exited the limo and took her dad's hand. The two got in place before the bridge and I arranged Aimee's long train. I was about to hurry across the bridge ahead of the procession and join Robert when I realized that Jenny and young Bill, Sarah and Jeff, and Mandy as flower girl were already beginning their walk. I was left stranded standing behind Aimee and Bill. What a fix they put me in. However, since I was taking pictures of the event, I edged off to the side and photographed them as they began their entry. Maybe it looked natural, I don't know. All I know is that I was embarrassed to be stuck in the middle of the processional. I snapped pictures the whole way in an effort to make it look like that's exactly where I wanted to be.

The ceremony itself was a very spiritually moving one. The minister had worked out the wording beforehand. Everyone witnessing the solemn affair commented later on how beautiful it was.

The reception was held in Green Mountain Falls at the Pub'n'Grub restaurant which has a mountain atmosphere created by large old logs and an enormous fireplace. Aimee and Robert had invited their friends from work and his relatives came from out of state. We'd invited all our friends including Joe and Monika from Valhalla, and some very special friends from Kansas City. The afternoon was spent sharing laughter and dancing; however, Robert and Joe were the only gentlemen who asked me to dance. I sat and talked with Carole Bourdo while watching Bill make the rounds on the dance floor. I think he was too excited to notice that he'd not danced with me the whole time.

The limousine returned and we saw Aimee and Robert off. They were going to Denver to spend the night, then fly off to Mexico the following morning. I was so happy for them. They looked to be so very much in love. Ah, young love, how beautiful it can be.

By the time Aimee and Robert got married, Jenny was wearing an engagement ring. She and young Bill were setting their date for October, 1995. My babies were growing up.

## SPIRIT OF THE STANDING STONES

While Robert and Aimee were sunning and swimming in Mexico, we closed on our new house. July 11th was the day we signed our names on the contract that gave us ownership of the house that came with the heavenly omen. Tuesday evening, Chu-Chu and I went over to the vacant place. I'd planned on doing a little cleaning before moving day, but the former owners had left it so spotless that there was little to do but put away some of the more fragile native and nature things I'd personally brought over. That evening it was just me and Chu who stayed the night. We slept on the bedroom floor and listened to our new home's steady heartbeat and rhythmic breathing. It seemed to be a good earth spot to have a home. It felt very sound and safe. It rested on solid bedrock.

On Wednesday, Sarah, Jenny, and Bill accompanied the

movers to the house. By evening, I had nearly every box unpacked and put away—all but my books, those I saved to savor the following day.

Life in the new place was not all as serene as the house itself was. Bill still had problems with depression spells and required a great deal of time talking on the phone with our new friend. When she came to visit, they'd spend more time working on easing his heart pains and life problems. During these times I felt very much alone, but couldn't express that in lieu of wanting to get Bill the help he felt he needed. I didn't want to sound like a selfish or jealous wife. Actually, I never had a jealous bone in my body, but I did feel resentment at times that he was spending so much time with our lady friend. Bill insisted that I should let him be free to follow his own guidance in regard to how he could best be helped. . .so that's what I did. What was especially hard on me was when he called our friend to tell her goodbye—he'd taken his gun and driven off. Not knowing if he was alive or dead was a real torment for me to go through.

At this same time, Bill began seeing a new massage therapist in Woodland Park. It seemed that Roxanne had a wonderfully effective technique for helping reduce the pain of broken hearts. Bill said she was good at what she called Trauma Release, and he raved about how much she was helping his aching heart. I was grateful for the alleged expertise, yet it seemed that, as time went on, Bill became more openly expressive to others about some very specific inadequacies he believed I had and he couldn't accept. I didn't find out about these until months later. At the time, I thought we were relating well with one another, especially since he was being treated by Roxanne and spending so much time with our other lady friend. Though we two were relating well on a surface level, his bouts of depression appeared to get more frequent and went into deeper states. I couldn't quite figure it with all the assistance he was getting from his two helpers, but their discussions were strictly confidential and I wasn't permitted to be a participant. This was what Bill insisted upon. He said he needed the privacy of their interaction and communications.

On the morning of Sunday, August 14th, Bill woke me early and called me outside. What a sight! A rolling mist of pearly clouds was snaking up the valley toward us. We watched it divide and circle in front of our property and then come around the back. I rushed inside, grabbed the camera and ran around the deck to look further down the valley. I was stopped dead in my tracks. A chill rippled up my spine. A shiver trembled through me. My eyes locked on a black image within the wavering clouds.

Down among the rocks below us was the very clear image of a man's head and shoulders. The image was dense black and, from elbow to elbow, was a half circle of rainbow light. Surrounding the entire image and rainbow aura was a second full rainbow circle enclosing the whole manifestation.

I stared and stared.

The black image never wavered. . .it seemed solid—three-dimensional. I got off four or five shots of it and hoped to God that they'd come out. What I saw was one of the most completely unexpected apparitions I'd ever witnessed.

I called for Bill to come around the deck.

When he arrived, the manifestation was slowly beginning to fade. He could still make it out and was absolutely amazed at how the man's form maintained its shape without undulating like the clouds outside the surrounding rainbow circle. Eventually the image and circles vanished. Bill returned to the house while I stood transfixed to the spot.

*What* was that?

*Who* was that?

*Why* was the *who* there?

At least I'd gotten some photos of it. If nobody believed what we'd seen, the photographs would verify the man in the standing stones for us.

An hour later we were sitting in the Gold Rush Casino eating breakfast. I'd excitedly explained the manifestation to Aimee and Robert, who were back to work. I think I may have been so cranked up over the incident that I might have appeared to be drinking my breakfast instead of eating it. No matter. We saw what we saw *before* we even entered the casino.

After breakfast, Bill stayed at the casino to visit with his new son-in-law while he tended bar and I left to browse through the remaining gift shops in Cripple Creek. I'd been looking for a certain type of small turquoise earrings and I found something very much like them in one of the jewelry shops. Returning to the Gold Rush, I met up with Bill and we left before being tempted to hand over our change to one of the flashy one-armed bandits.

That evening, when I unpacked the few items I'd bought in Cripple Creek, the earrings were nowhere to be found. The receipt was there, but no tissue-wrapped earrings. I took the receipt and set it on Bill's desk so I'd be reminded to call the shop in the morning to see if they were left on the counter by mistake. I felt disappointed that they were missing. I'd spent many months looking for them.

Monday morning brought a new manifestation for us to wonder over. On the center of the dining room table was a wad of thickly folded tissue. I picked it up and unwrapped the paper. There, within, was my pair of earrings! They had appeared out of nowhere. They were not there the night before when we went to bed. They were nowhere to be found last night. Yet, this morning, sitting all by themselves on a bare table, were those earrings.

Not to complain, mind you. I whispered swift words of thanks to whoever had been thoughtful enough to manifest them back to me. Yes, for the little things in life I'd learned to be very, very thankful.

On Friday, August 26th, Sarah picked up my photographs from town. I was nearly jumping out of my skin to see my Spirit of the Standing Stones. I flipped photo after photo and didn't find him. I looked to Sarah. "Are these all the photos there were?"

She shrugged. She just picked up the set. She didn't count them to see if they were all there.

Again I flashed through the stack like a crack card dealer. No image of a man could be found. . .only a shadowy star outline with an extremely faint yellow circlet showing.

A wry smile tipped the corner of my mouth. Oh well, isn't that always the way? Isn't that always the way when you want to prove something really happened?

Bill wasn't surprised. "When you were out there taking those pictures, didn't I hear you say something about using it in the *Bittersweet* book?"

"Yeah. I definitely wanted it to be published in the book." He grinned then. "There you go. There's your answer."

"Answer?"

"Whoever was down there that morning obviously read your mind and didn't want the image published." Then he chuckled, "Maybe he's just like you."

I frowned. "Me?"

"Yeah. Doesn't like publicity."

A camera-shy spirit? Yeah. Yeah, I could relate to that one.

Through meditation I learned that the apparition among the standing stones manifested for the purpose of providing Bill and me with encouragement. It'd been a long time since we'd heard any form of direct communication from our Advisors. The appearance of the spirit's opaque silhouette and the extended amount of time it held solid within the swirling mist served to reinforce our Advisors' companionship and continued state of attention to our affairs. In my mind it wasn't so much as a sign that they were still with us, but more of a cautious statement. STEP CAREFULLY. TREAD WISELY. WE'RE KEEPING A CLOSE WATCH ON YOUR DEVELOPING SITUATION. This message comforted me in many ways. It was especially meaningful and personally encouraging. It meant that I could and would survive this stress-filled and lonely time. It meant there was more to endure, yet endure I would.

A few days later, one of the three massage therapists Bill was seeing wanted to show him the land she'd acquired. He informed me that the two of them were going to walk the property and then have a picnic lunch. He was gone all day.

I never asked Bill why he didn't invite me to go with him—I'd stopped asking intrusive questions like that a long time ago. By simply *accepting* instead of *asking*, I found a path to peace instead of confrontation. Hiding the hurts helped keep a measure of harmony in our home. I'd become an expert at hiding the pains of my heart. Nobody saw them. . .nobody sensed them. *Nobody.*

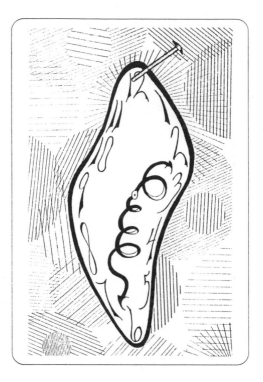

# TIME WARP

Monday, August 29th, marked the day when Sarah got her first official job. She'd gone over to the Gold Rush Casino to put in an application. Aimee spotted her and went over to chat. Before anyone knew it, Sarah was hired as the Golden Griddle's breakfast and lunch cook.

This was scary stuff for Sarah. She brought home the menu to memorize as fast as she could because the main cook was leaving his position soon. He was moving out of state and had to train Sarah in a hurry. Sarah was not pleased about this rush, rush situation. Sarah is not and never was a rush, rush person.

As it turned out, the cook was in too much of a rush to train Sarah at all. She ended up working in the kitchen as a cook's assistant and spent her days washing mountain-high piles of potatoes, cooking meatloaf, making salads and soups, trimming meats, and baking rolls. Her behind-the-scene tales either made us laugh ourselves right off our chairs or they made us gag and run for the nearest sink. She didn't take long to reach an intolerable stage at her job. She didn't take long to begin keeping her eyes open for something else. She didn't take long to begin working upstairs at the casino's Best Western Hotel. And she didn't take long to have her first experience with the hotel's playful little lady ghost. Then her behind-the-scene tales were quite different. Oh yes, they were tales of a quite different kind. The day after Sarah was hired on at the Gold Rush Casino, Bill and I had a fair day together. He did errands in town and returned in a better-than-usual mood. I worked on cleaning the house during my breaks from writing this journal. But this particular Tuesday, this August 30th, seemed different somehow. I picked up something unusual in the air. The atmosphere seemed charged, but not electrically-speaking; it was more like an altered vibration or a dimensional shift was trying to occur. Off and on during the day I found myself going out on the deck and just standing there trying to discern what it was I was picking up on. The sensation wasn't one I was accustomed to. It wasn't one I could readily identify.

In the evening, when Bill and I were sitting on the couch watching a movie, a great flash of light speared into the living room from the bank of big windows behind us. The light was more of a blue strobe type. . .and the electricity went out. I rose from the couch to light the candles and Bill went for a couple flashlights. Jenny walked from the kitchen into the front entryway and I was up in a raised room looking out tall and narrow windows. Simultaneously Jenny and I saw a brilliant orb flash in the sky near us.

"OH!" she exclaimed.

"Wow!" I grinned. "Jenny! You *see* that?" I called down to her.

"Yeah! What *was* that?"

"Lightning," came Bill's reply.

"No *way*!" Jenny shouted back.

I reinforced Jenny's opinion. "No way is right, Jenny. That was no lightning. That definitely was not lightning."

Bill came to the window. "What was it then? What did you guys see out there?"

I hesitated. "Something. We saw something."

He pushed. "What're your feelings then?"

I stared up at the spot in the sky. "The same feelings I got from the first flash that came right through our windows at a horizontal angle. My feelings are that Starman used their technology to make an atmospheric adjustment around us. I've been feeling a weirdness to it all day long. I was looking right up at the night sky when that second flash came. It appeared to have come from a circular opening of some kind. It was perfectly round." I thought a moment. "Nobody heard any thunder after either of the flashes, did they?"

Jenny quickly responded. "There wasn't any thunder after either of the flashes."

Bill agreed.

So did I.

Shortly thereafter, strong promptings kept returning over and over in my mind. . .strong thoughts. . .directives. . .to finally secure that getaway cabin we'd been waiting for seven years to get for me. And a week later, we began looking for my little woodland place that would finally align with my own vibrations. . .the little place where I could finally find a small measure of peace and solace in nature.

We celebrated Jenny's twenty-fifth birthday on Friday, September 2nd, and on Wednesday, the 14th, she made a monumental step back into independence. . .she went back to work at the Gold Rush Casino. On the 14th she became my Little Braveheart. Going back to work after being gone for nine months was an extremely difficult move for Jen. What served as a strong impetus was the fact that she and her young Bill were moving into a rental in Cripple Creek and her added income would certainly help them have an easier life. Young Bill had secured a job at one of the casinos and needed to move up from Colorado Springs. Likewise, if Jenny lived right there in Cripple Creek she could walk back and forth to work. It was a difficult decision for her to make. She worried about what her coworkers would say, if they'd question her about the robbery of a year ago. She felt ill at ease returning to the scene of the crime, fearful that others would look askance at her. She was anxious about the Cripple Creek officers that frequently have business in the casinos; she didn't especially want to see any of them. But most of all she worried about an officer coming in and handing her a subpoena to appear as a witness at the gunman's trial that was coming up. Many of the casino employees had been getting these. Jenny did once, but the trial was continued. It frightened her to death to think she'd have to face the gunman and sit before a court filled with gawkers, telling about the robbery plans she'd overheard and pointing out the gunman. Yet despite these fears and worries, Jenny straightened her back and returned to work. Jan, the shift manager, had already expressed to me that she'd be happy to have Jenny back at work. Other employees wanted to see her back too. So back she went and she hasn't been sorry. My Little Braveheart is one fine little lady.

Sarah's birthday came on a day when many other events happened in our lives. It was the first day of autumn. When Sarah turned nineteen we closed on my little getaway cabin. Her birthday coincided with me finally obtaining the one thing Bill and I had been talking about getting for over seven years. It was a day when one of my long-time dreams finally came true. And I was bursting with joy over it. The fact that I'd actually gotten the cabin didn't seem real, not at first. I'd waited for so long, always having to put our money on other, more important, needs; putting my great need for it off year after year, thinking it was only a pipe dream I was fantasizing about. Yet in my private thoughts, I knew that it would one day be a reality for me. It had to be. It just had to. Without having such a place of peace for me to escape from telephones and the television and the noise of talking, I felt like a fish out of water or a caged hawk. My vibrations don't align with the world at large or with people in general or with mechanical sounds and noise. I have to have the silence of the woods, the whispers of the wind through the high pines, the language of nature. And so this was what could only soothe my weary soul. This was what could only give me solace and, in the end, *some* sense of love.

The final event that marked Sarah's 19th birthday came late in the evening after our electricity for the entire mountain residential region went out for a few seconds. We didn't think much of it because it happens often enough for various reasons, but what made it remarkable was when Aimee called us the following day.

"Did your electricity go out last night?" she asked.

"Yeah, but for only a few seconds," I said.

"Mom! You'll never guess what!" She was so excited about what happened at her and Robert's place.

"What?" I laughed. "What happened?"

"When the electricity at our place went out last night we didn't think anything about it until this morning."

"What happened this morning?"

"You're not going to believe this."

I laughed again. "Try me."

"All our clocks were twenty minutes FAST!"

# BENEATH THE ALPINE MOON

On Sunday, September 25th, we moved some of our odd pieces of unwanted furniture into the cabin. It felt absolutely wonderful to put my collection of native effects and nature finds in a place where they seemed to naturally belong. The dwelling had a powerful Sacred Ground feel to it. It felt just as though it was resting in the warm palm of God's hand. At least that's precisely what my flash of vision was when I first saw it. And the formidable energy that permeated the land brought forth a strong sense of complete safety and protection.

And so it was that I joyfully filled the place with varying elements that aligned with the primal essence of my being; cherished gifts sent by my kind and thoughtful readers, precious nature finds I'd discovered on woodswalks, and some that came from very special friends during their own forest journeys.

Overnight, the entire interior of the cabin became a frozen season of autumn. Colorful leaves were set in nooks and crannies, boughs of red and gold lay like pine boughs framing the bedroom dresser, bright branches grace Carole Bourdo's painting of No-Eyes' cabin, a grapevine wreath interwoven with brilliant maple leaves hangs on the wall, and the heady scent of cedar incense permeates every room. Autumn. My little cabin is frozen in time. . .autumn time.

There's no fancy furniture there. We borrowed the well-used love seat from the main house, my reading chair, a cedar chest, and a rocker. In the kitchen area is a metal folding table that serves my dining needs, yet mostly, I eat while sitting and reading or watching the fire. After twilight, electric lights are a rarity. By nature, I much prefer my five candles and two oil pots, for these give adequate illumination for my needs and the tranquil atmosphere soothes my very weary soul.

One room contains my work area and bookcases which are filled with special volumes and native/nature collectibles. One shelf holds the music player and a few favorite CDs. Green plants are beginning to grace the floor beneath the window that looks out past the birdfeeder to high mountain ridges beyond.

The second room is the bedroom where a hand-stitched quilt and fur covers the dark pine bed. Again, autumn abounds in all its colorful splendor there. Even in slumber, the beauty of Autumn's Spirit surrounds me.

Three rooms and a bath. That's my little place in the pines beneath the alpine moon. And what a palace it is.

Outside, pines, firs, spruce, and aspens surround the small cabin like living sentinels. Down in the forest, I chose a special place to make my Prayer Circle. Now I've worn a footpath to it and, several nights a week, I'm out there for at least an hour, lost in prayer. While there, Chu-Chu runs free in the forest, yet she seems to have developed a routine that has amazed me. She patrols a twenty-foot perimeter around the Prayer Circle and, if she goes farther to check out a sound in the woods, she races back into the Prayer Circle to check on me before circling the perimeter again. If she detects tears in my eyes, she'll lick them off before running back to her perimeter patrol line. She does this routing until I finish my prayers and call her to join me for the walk back up to the cabin. My little Cheyenne has been quite a surprise. In more ways than I can count, she's been my companion, my source of affectionately-given pure love, my devoted protector, my source of frequent laughter, and my friend. Oh, how I continually offer prayers of thanksgiving that she called so strongly to me that day I searched for books in the mall. Daily I'm thankful for such a warm and loving friend. And now, now Cheyenne has a tiny sister to play with. My dear friend's Yorkshire Terrier gave birth to four miniature pups. The only female was earmarked for me. I named her Pinecone for obvious reasons—she'll never be bigger than one. So now Cheyenne and Pinecone stay with me at the cabin. While Pinecone sleeps beneath my chin, Cheyenne is proud to keep her guard at my bedroom door. While Pinecone slumbers in my reading chair, Cheyenne walks the woods with me and patrols her self-designated perimeter of my Prayer Circle. While Pinecone sleeps on my lap while I type, Cheyenne is content to curl up at my feet beneath the table.

Daily I'm thankful for my two little four-legged loved ones. Daily I'm thankful for my little peaceful place beneath the alpine moon. . .without it I would surely wither away like a dried autumn leaf. Without it I would surely die.

## AND THEN THERE WAS ONE

After I obtained the little cabin, life back at home didn't improve. Bill and I had previously worked out an amicable getaway schedule for me to spend time at the cabin. This schedule was needed in order for me to gear down when I first got over there and then ease into the more harmonious vibrations of the cabin and surrounding woods. This gave me a couple days to rejuvenate and spend golden communion time out in the silent forest for an effective alignment with nature. In this manner, my spirit became completely restful and this, in turn, heightened my sensitivity in order to reach the more receptive state required for the purpose of furthering my work. Some days away were needed for physical rest, others for emotional distance from life's daily troubles and resulting stress. Whatever the need, the block of time effectively served me well. And, back at home, Bill thought it extremely interesting to play out the bachelor role while I was gone for a few days. He'd immediately slipped into a pattern of playful banter with calling the cabin "your" house and he called our joint house "his" place. And we both joked about it. . .until he began to feel insecure in our love because I was gone a few days a week. He let himself slide into a convincing belief that I didn't love him anymore.

So then the rules changed on me. He and some of our friends thought it best for me to return my typewriter to the main house so I'd be home with Bill more. This, I suppose, was meant to equate my physical presence with my love for him.

I couldn't believe what I was asked to do. After waiting for more than seven years to have my need of the cabin met, I was suddenly expected to stay at home to prove my love.

What? A grown woman, older than any of those around her, isn't allowed to fulfill her greatest need? She can't express her individuality through experiencing the solitude she'd so desperately sought for her spirit's peace? I felt humiliated. I felt as though everyone treated me like a truant child being pulled back into school. Yet, in deference to Bill's emotional needs, I brought back the typewriter and worked at home. I did this because Bill went into a period of raging at me about being away from him. I did this because, after his outbursts, he stormed out of the house with his gun and swore I'd never see him again. After sitting in the dark living room and listening intently to the scanner for the police transmission of his death, or hear a scrambled communication and think it might be talk of his discovered demise, I was in torment with the anxiety. And time after time he'd return, walk through the living room, enter the bedroom and close the door.

After several more of these repeated incidents, I was beginning to lose the predictability of our relationship. His mood swings happened so swiftly that I frequently felt frightened. Gunplay, especially when it was mixed with alcohol, was not part of my makeup and he carried his around much too often for me to be restful in its presence.

At this same time, other issues began to cause problems in our relationship, all based on various new inadequacies that

Bill thought he perceived in me that he could not accept. It appeared that, no matter what I did to try to please him or change to suit him, I still wasn't how he wanted me to be. I was beginning to feel like I was being chipped away at, worn down, always criticized for being me.

One evening when I was over at the cabin, he came over and stood in the office doorway. He merely stared at me. His jacket was zipped up, something he only did when his gun was concealed there. And I was scared of what I didn't see in his eyes. The Ice Man was there instead of the Bill I knew. He left without incident. The next night he came to the cabin door. I was fearful and refused him entrance. I asked him to go home and call me on the phone so we could discuss whatever he wanted to talk about.

These situations were never the norm for our past relationship. They'd become something out of a dark dreamscape that grew into an incredulous living nightmare. The nightmares came more frequently and began to run together. Some nights I fled to the cabin and locked myself in, for it was there that I had a variety of protective measures I could depend on if the need ever arose. This thought deeply devastated me because I knew that Bill would never do intentional harm, yet his tirades frightened me and his complaints about me grew more frequent and animated. And I was crushed to hear that he'd been complaining about me to family and friends for many months before he'd brought them to me. What did I do? What did I do that was so wrong?

Was finally obtaining the cabin I so desperately needed for so long what did it? I'd like to blame it on something touchable and impersonal like that, yet I know it isn't so. It appeared that I'd not been adequate in various critical ways for many, many years and I never knew it.

I'd stayed in the relationship during the years he sought out others to fulfill his emotional needs. I'd stayed and been there for him, yet he never saw me standing off to the side waiting for him to put out his arms to me rather than another. I'd hung in and endured the torment of listening to the police scanner, always pacing in stress-filled anxiety, wondering when the officers were going to knock on our door. I remained with him after he convinced himself I didn't love him anymore and allowed myself to be pulled away from the cabin and back home to where he could take comfort in my constant presence. I stayed despite his objections to my only friend calling me on the phone while I was home. This, he claimed, took me away from his time with me. And when I was at home with him, he'd resent me being downstairs in the office working on this book and rage at me for not being upstairs with him. And I continued to hear his complaints regarding his nonacceptance of my perceived faults and real needs. I lost my appetite. I was down to one hundred pounds.

Maybe I did have all those faults he complained to others about. All I know is that I hung in there until the tips of my fingers were about to break off before I gave our relationship three more final last-ditch efforts to save it. These failed due to my alleged faults being too great for him to overlook. All I know is that I gave and gave until I felt I had nothing more of me to give. . .until I had nothing more of me at all. Finally the tips of my fingers broke off trying to hold on and it was with a broken heart that I threw in the towel. I finally had to find a way to preserve the small piece of me that I saw looking back from the mirror.

By the time Christmas came our relationship had plunged into such a fragmented state of deterioration that neither Bill nor I was in any kind of holiday mood. It was the first year we didn't bother putting up a Christmas tree. The house and cabin had a bit of holly branches placed about to mark the season; other than that, the two places seemed barren amidst the gaily decorated and festive dwellings of family and friends.

On a Monday, January 23, 1995, Bill went to see an attorney. The following day we went together. Using one attorney to handle our new legal affair posed no difficulty because neither of us wanted to hurt any longer. Dividing up our property would be fair—from the heart—because our prime goal was to part friends and forever remain so. We still reserve a special place in our hearts for the other. We still care very much for each other. These two cherished aspects of a long relationship are what we've strived to preserve before it became too late to save them. I hope and pray that we'll always remain friends. As of this writing our separate plans are being formulated.

Bill has chosen to keep residing in our formerly-shared house where he's in close proximity to the girls' places. He and I are in daily communication. For his early birthday present I bought him a Keeshond pup and Bill takes him nearly everywhere he goes. Bill expressed a sentiment that he wished me to convey to my readers—to please not be judgmental of either of us.

On Thursday, January 26, 1995, I moved into the little cabin-in-the-woods. . .my needs are not more than that. I plan on reaching out and touching my readers by participating in frequent booksignings for the next couple of years, for this one aspect of my work—more than any other—gives me great joy and warms my heart.

My work will keep me busy until I ease into its final phase and, until then. . .I look forward to the sweet essence of Grandmother Earth's compassionate spirit to comfort and heal my weary soul.

Because of continuing death-threat letters and the more recently manifested premonition dreams of kidnapping incidents that contain vivid location details that were verified by doing some extensive investigative footwork, I currently have a live-in security person who is with me twenty-four hours a day. The underlying cause for this situation is a grave confoundment to my mind, yet the Knowing within me confirms the reason—the causal basis—as being one aspect that signals the growing negativity and decline of the Times that No-Eyes prophesied so long ago. Her words dealt with the aspect of human psychology during the beginning of the Phoenix Days when a great percentage of the populace would lose all respect for what is right and begin giving free rein to their baser emotions by acting on them without regard to conscience or consequence. In short, people would begin losing it—snapping. They wouldn't hesitate to take action on their negative thoughts and imaginings. And so I do understand the increased incidents of these threats that come my way by way of letter and shimmering, crystal-clear premonition dreams. My intellect understands. . .my heart does not.

Considering how this journal ends, I suppose the title proved more than prophetic too. I had no idea it would end this way between Bill and me when the journal began. I sincerely ask that you continue praying for us. Though Bill and I came here with separate and unique missions, we're still obligated to deal with everyday living situations and relationships that don't always work out for the best.

Bittersweet.

Yes, how bittersweet life has turned out to be. Yet the fact remains, the sweet can only be truly savored after one has passed a measure of bitters over the tongue. Strength comes from experiencing and surviving life's cup of bitters.

Bittersweet.

It has a rare beauty all its own. Though it be an enigmatic beauty—one of profound contrasts—it has beauty all the same. To survive its message is to understand its beauty. And so it is that branches of the bright, berried bittersweet have always graced my fireplace mantle. And so it is that a single sprig of it—so fragile, yet powerful—will always be carried deep within my heart.

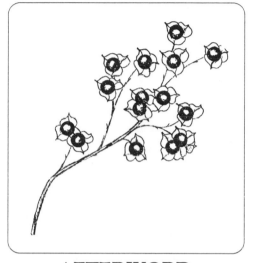

# AFTERWORD

Sitting at my typewriter, I glance out the window before me. The flurry of activity outside is too urgent to ignore. Black and grey squirrels, tiny chipmunks and an array of birds are scurrying about the ground. A light snowfall has begun to cover the scattered seeds and grain. Yet I've always cared for them. How is it that they haven't learned that I'll put out more food for them if their current supply is no longer visible to them? The panic continues despite the fact that I'll soon bring them fresh seed and grain to feed from. How is it that they don't remember this?

Turning my head, my gaze rested on the desk calendar. It is May, May of 1995. And it has been exactly thirteen years since I first encountered No-Eyes. Thirteen. Thirteen long years. That realization was holding me spellbound as I again shifted my gaze toward the window.

Snow. So new and fresh. Perfect crystals slowly turning in their gentle, silent fall to earth. So peaceful is the sight. So filled with raw beauty. So tranquil and pure. All of these attributes benevolently gift the scene outside my window with a new and altered view—a changed perspective—of reality. It is changed, yet beautiful all the same. It is different than before, yet still pure and benevolent. So, how is it that the little ground critters have become frantic because of it?

These thoughts reminded me of all the changes that took place in my life within the past thirteen years. Then I related my life to those of others who have struggled through daily problems while still cherishing the bright and shining light of truth within their hearts. Upon the ground we toil and struggle for such basic needs as food and shelter and, much like my tiny critters outside my window, we too often forget that a change of scene, or perspective, or view of reality doesn't necessarily shatter our elemental faith. Changes come in many forms. Changes are the stuff Reality is made of.

To acknowledge change is to recognize the Big Picture. This Picture is the primal essence of Reality's basic composition. . . change. Vibration. Frequency. All constant, undulating motion. Though the combinations interchange, meld and interchange again like a child's turning kaleidoscope, the basic components remain the same. And it is God who holds all the components in His hand. Therefore, what I'm trying to convey with all of this fundamental fact is that: No matter *what*, we are *still* in God's hands. Our surroundings can change, the topographic view of our homeland can alter, pieces of reality can move about and interchange, yet God still holds all the Parts of the Whole. He is the DNA of our Reality.

Clearly, I've allowed one thought to lead to another and another still, yet this is how my process functions during the frequent times of contemplation. Why these specific thoughts now? At the Eleventh Hour of putting *Bittersweet* to bed? The chapter on Revelations spurred them on.

I realize that certain points within that chapter may cause a wide range of reactions. Yet what is paramount for us to remain focused on is the infinite benevolence of God and how much He loves and cares for each of us. Though our surroundings may change, we are all still His childern. Though we are given new perspectives on Reality, He is still our loving Father. He will leave open a "living" Lifeline for earth's future. I will relate more of this aspect when I write the third novel of the Starborn Trilogy that began with *The Seventh Mesa.* Until then, cherish every cell of the Truth that pulses within your hearts, live those truths, love the love our Father has for us and, most of all, know that He will continue to care and provide for us.

Now I'm going outside to provide for those little critters who have forgotten how much I love them.

Hampton Roads publishes books on
metaphysical, spiritual, health-related, and
general interest subjects. Would you like to be notified
as we publish new books in your area of interest?
If you would like a copy of our latest catalog, just call toll-free,
(800) 766-8009, or send your name and address to:

Hampton Roads Publishing Company, Inc.
976 Norfolk Square
Norfolk, VA 23502